AF621640

Archaeological Heritage Policies and Management Structures

Proceedings of the XVII UISPP World Congress (1–7 September 2014, Burgos, Spain)

Volume 15 / Sessions A15a, A15b, A15c

Edited by

Erika M. Robrahn-González,
Friedrich Lüth, Abdoulaye Cámara, Pascal Depaepe,
Asya Engovatova, Ranjana Ray and Vidula Jayswal

Archaeopress Archaeology

ARCHAEOPRESS PUBLISHING LTD
Gordon House
276 Banbury Road
Oxford OX2 7ED

www.archaeopress.com

ISBN 978 1 78491 738 8
ISBN 978 1 78491 739 5 (e-Pdf)

© Archaeopress, UISPP and authors 2017

VOLUME EDITORS: Erika M. Robrahn-González, Friedrich Lüth, Abdoulaye Cámara, Pascal Depaepe, Asya Engovatova, Ranjana Ray & Vidula Jayswal

SERIES EDITOR: The board of UISPP

SERIES PROPERTY: UISPP – International Union of Prehistoric and Protohistoric Sciences

Proceedings of the XVII World UISPP Congress, Burgos (Spain)
September 1st – 7th 2014

KEYWORDS IN THIS VOLUME: Archaeology; Heritage; Policies; Management Structures

UISPP PROCEEDINGS SERIES is a printed on demand and an open access publication, edited by UISPP through Archaeopress

BOARD OF UISPP: Jean Bourgeois (President), Luiz Oosterbeek (Secretary-General), François Djindjian (Treasurer), Ya-Mei Hou (Vice President), Marta Arzarello (Deputy Secretary-General). The Executive Committee of UISPP also includes the Presidents of all the international Scientific Commissions (www.uispp.org)

BOARD OF THE XVII WORLD CONGRESS OF UISPP: Eudald Carbonell (Secretary-General), Robert Sala I Ramos, Jose Maria Rodriguez Ponga (Deputy Secretary-Generals)

All rights reserved. No part of this book may be reproduced, or transmitted, in any form or by any means, electronic, mechanical, photocopying or otherwise, without the prior written permission of the copyright owners.

This book is available direct from Archaeopress or from our website www.archaeopress.com

Contents

CULTURAL RESOURCES, MANAGEMENT, PUBLIC POLICY, PEOPLE'S AWARENESS AND SUSTAINABLE DEVELOPMENT
Session 15 C

List of Figures and Tables

ARCHAEOLOGICAL HERITAGE POLICIES AND MANAGEMENT STRUCTURES
Session 15 A

Z. Domingos: Public policies for the management of the Angolan archaeological heritage

S. L. Macamo and L. Adamowicz: The Legal Protection of Archaeological Heritage in Mozambique (1994-2014)

MANAGEMENT AND USE OF SCIENCE DATA FROM PREVENTIVE ARCHAEOLOGY: QUALITY CONTROL
Session 15 B

A. Koehler: Quality management organisation in Inrap (France)

P. Depaepe: Quality control in preventive archaeology in France: a review of the question

A. Engovatova: Archaeology in Russia today – the system of scientific control over the quality of rescue archaeology work

K. K. Siméon and F. Guédé Yiodé: Trois cas de prospections relatifs à des diagnostics archéologiques en Côte d'Ivoire (2008-2010): les entreprises d'extraction minière levier pour un nouvel ordre archéologique en Côte d'Ivoire?

CULTURAL RESOURCES, MANAGEMENT, PUBLIC POLICY, PEOPLE'S AWARENESS AND SUSTAINABLE DEVELOPMENT

Session 15 C

A. Basu: A study of the Archaeological sites of the Birbhum District, Bengal – Its management and sustainable development

D. K. Mondal: A Study of Prehistoric Cultural Heritage and Management in Odisha, India

K. Chakraborty, D. K. Mondal and R. Ray: Heritage of skill in making clay ornaments in India

B. Bhattacharyya: Mask of Chhau – A Tribal Heritage through the Ages in West Bengal: An Ethno-Archaeological Study in Charida Group of People

Foreword to the XVII UISPP Congress Proceedings Series Edition

Luiz Oosterbeek
Secretary-General

UISPP has a long history, starting with the old International Association of Anthropology and Archaeology, back in 1865, until the foundation of UISPP itself in Bern, in 1931, and its growing relevance after WWII, from the 1950's. We also became members of the International Council of Philosophy and Human Sciences, associate of UNESCO, in 1955.

In its XIVth world congress in 2001, in Liège, UISPP started a reorganization process that was deepened in the congresses of Lisbon (2006) and Florianópolis (2011), leading to its current structure, solidly anchored in more than twenty-five international scientific commissions, each coordinating a major cluster of research within six major chapters: Historiography, methods and theories; Culture, economy and environments; Archaeology of specific environments; Art and culture; Technology and economy; Archaeology and societies.

The XVIIth world congress of 2014, in Burgos, with the strong support of Fundación Atapuerca and other institutions, involved over 1700 papers from almost 60 countries of all continents. The proceedings, edited in this series but also as special issues of specialized scientific journals, will remain as the most important outcome of the congress.

Research faces growing threats all over the planet, due to lack of funding, repressive behavior and other constraints. UISPP moves ahead in this context with a strictly scientific programme, focused on the origins and evolution of humans, without conceding any room to short term agendas that are not root in the interest of knowledge.

In the long run, which is the terrain of knowledge and science, not much will remain from the contextual political constraints, as severe or dramatic as they may be, but the new advances into understanding the human past and its cultural diversity will last, this being a relevant contribution for contemporary and future societies.

This is what UISPP is for, and this is also why we are currently engaged in contributing for the relaunching of Human Sciences in their relations with social and natural sciences, namely collaborating with the International Year of Global Understanding, in 2016, and with the World Conference of the Humanities, in 2017.

The next congress of UISPP, in Paris (2018), will confirm this route.

Foreword

Erika M. Robrahn-González
President of the UISPP Scientific Commission 'Archaeological Heritage Policies and Management Structures'
erika@documentocultural.net

This volume is composed of articles referring to the analyses and reflections accomplished during the XVII World Congress of the UISPP (*Union de Sciences Préhistoriques et Protohistoriques / Union of Pre-historic and Historic Sciences*) that took place in Burgos, Spain, in September of 2014. This is the first publication of the Scientific Commission 'Archaeological Heritage Policies and Management Structures', which began its activities in 2013.

This Scientific Commission's goal is to exchange experiences on archaeological heritage policies and management structures on a global level. Models, good practices, and solutions to individual sites and landscapes help to develop heritage management through better understanding among specialists while respecting the regional, national, and global diversities and individualities. The interdependence and the effects for science are part of the considerations and special attention is given to the integrated approach of heritage management, local needs and specificities, and science.

Recovering the concept of '*Think globally, act locally*', the aim of this Scientific Commission is also to analyse Archaeology's role in the 21st century regarding the way in which people must live together to ensure sustainability and a better understanding and full awareness of natural and cultural tradition.

In Burgos/2014, the first world congress in which this Scientific Commission took part, sessions aimed at different themes related to management, valuing and preservation of archaeological heritage were developed. The chapters that follow are related to three of these sessions:

Session '*Archaeological Heritage Policies and Management Strategies*', where international management models focused on legislation, public policies, management systems, and institutional contexts for research were presented.

Session '*Management and use of science data from preventive archaeology: quality control*', where reflections on the range of quality control in projects of applied science, including environmental topics and social standards were developed. The session's main goals were: to analyse and compare different international quality control models; to list best solutions and good practices; and to propose new criteria for preventive archaeology.

Session '*Cultural resources, management, public policy, people's awareness and sustainable development*', focused on local traditional crafts, many of which exist continuously from prehistoric period to present day. Work presented in this session analysed public policy models for the preservation of such heritage, people's awareness of the cultural resources and their management, with emphasis on sustainable development, especially from a background of a changed world perspective.

The following chapters bring perspectives of archaeological heritage management in various countries and continents. We hope, with this, to contribute to the exchange of experiences, the sharing of solutions, and the broadening of Archaeology's role in the sustainable development of people as its final goal.

ARCHAEOLOGICAL HERITAGE POLICIES AND MANAGEMENT STRUCTURES

Session 15 A

Edited by

Erika M. Robrahn-González, Friedrich Lüth and Abdoulaye Cámara

Public policies for the management of the Angolan archaeological heritage

Ziva Domingos
Direcção Nacional dos Museus de Angola, Rua Major Kanhangulo, 77, C.P. 1267 Luanda
zivado@hotmail.com

Abstract
After 30 years marked by war, Angola as a young nation is making efforts to boost its development in order to provide a quality life to its people. To achieve this, the Angolan Government, since the end of the war in 2002, launched the challenge of diversifying its economy by using all available resources in various areas of economic, social and cultural life. It is in this perspective that the Angolan public cultural policy adopted in 2011, recognizes the cultural and natural heritage, especially the archaeological heritage as one of the pillars of sustainable development of Angola with immediate effects on the internal cohesion of local communities in building a united nation and prosperous. Despite the existence of a rich and diverse archaeological heritage (rock art sites, burial archaeological sites, museum collection, etc.) and taking into account the threats due to the Angola's economic growth, this ideal can only be achieved if in fact the public policies for managing this heritage are consolidated, since the training of managers, the reinforcement of measures for protection, preservation and management of sites, the development of research and promotion consistent policies, the development of decentralized and participative management strategies that involve not only local authorities but especially local communities and other civil society partners.

Keywords
Angola, Public Policies, Archeological Heritage, Local Communities, Sustainable Development

Résumé
Après 30 ans marqués par la guerre, l'Angola en tant que jeune nation, est en train de déployer des efforts pour booster son développement dans le but d'améliorer la qualité de vie de sa population. Pour y arriver, le gouvernement angolais, depuis la fin de la guerre en 2002, s'est lancé le défi de diversifier son économie en utilisant toutes les ressources disponibles dans les diverses sphères de la vie économique, sociale et culturelle. C'est dans cette perspective que la politique culturelle publique de l'Angola, approuvée en 2011, reconnaît le patrimoine culturel et naturel, plus spécifiquement le patrimoine archéologique comme un de piliers du développement durable de l'Angola avec des effets immédiats sur la cohésion interne de communautés locales, construisant ainsi une nation unie et prospère. Malgré l'existence d'un patrimoine archéologique riche et varié (sites d'arts rupestres, sites d'archéologie funéraire, collections muséales, etc.) et en prenant en compte les menaces dues à la croissance économique de l'Angola, l'idéal serait atteint si et seulement si les politiques publiques de gestion de ce patrimoine seraient consolidées, a partir de la formation de gestionnaires de sites, le renforcement de mesures de protection, de préservation et de gestion de sites, le développement de la recherche et la promotion de politiques cohérentes, le développement de stratégies de gestion décentralisées et participatives qui impliquent non seulement les autorités locales mais surtout les communautés locales et les autres partenaires de la société civile.

Mots-clés
Angola, Politiques publiques, Patrimoine archéologique, Communautés locales, Développement durable

Introduction

Since its independence in 1975, Angola as a young nation is making efforts to boost its development in order to provide a quality life to its people, more especially when the country became peaceful in 2002 after 30 years of civil war. From that moment, the Angolan Government launched itself the challenge of diversifying its economy by using all the available resources in the economic, social and cultural areas. It is in this perspective, that the social and cultural sectors became one of the

Government priorities. That is why the Angolan Government adopted in 2011 its public cultural policy which recognizes the cultural and natural heritage, especially the archaeological heritage, as one of the pillars of sustainable development of Angola with immediate effects on the internal cohesion of local communities in building a united nation and prosperous. Despite the existence of a rich and diverse archaeological heritage (rock art sites, burial Archaeology sites, museum collection, etc.), the main challenge is how this heritage can really contribute to the sustainable development of Angola. As Mr. Yambo (one of the former directors of the National Institute of Cultural Heritage) said: 'It's a real challenge to work in this delicate field of archaeological research, especially in a country that has no support structures to supply what is essential to make a success of this type of work' (Yambo>VAC, 2009: 8). This ideal of development through the heritage management requires strong public policies which really address issues related to the training of managers, the reinforcement of measures for protection, preservation and management of sites, the development of research and promotion consistent policies, the development of decentralized and participative management strategies that involve not only local authorities but especially local communities and other civil society partners.

In considering the challenges faced by the Angolan Heritage Institutions, this paper entitled: 'Public Policies for the Management of the Angolan Archeological Heritage' presents some reflections regarding these policies in looking at the legislation, the organizational structure and some of the activities which have been implemented to improve the current situation by opening new perspectives and considering the fact that there are still a lot of challenges to be faced.

Public policies for the management of the Angolan archeological heritage: legislation and organizational structure

The first part of this paper presents a critical analysis point of view for the public policies regarding the safeguarding, enhancement, promotion, communication and dissemination of the Angolan cultural heritage through legal instruments and existing institutions in emphasizing the management of the archaeological heritage, starting from the first years of accession of Angola to the independence up to now.

Legal Framework

Cultural Policy

Before analyzing what the Angolan Cultural Policy declares in regard to the management of cultural heritage, it seems necessary to look a little bit at what the Constitution of the Republic of Angola[1] highlights regarding the preservation and promotion of the national culture. The Constitution of the Republic of Angola expressed clearly in its articles 79 and 87, the right of access of any Angolan citizen to Culture and, more specifically, his right to the conservation, enhancement of historic, cultural and artistic heritage and the State's duty to preserve this heritage, in these terms:

Article 79:

'The State shall promote the access to literacy, education, culture and sport to all, encouraging the participation of many private agents in its implementation, in accordance with law'.

Article 87:

'Citizens and communities are entitled to respect, promote and preserve of their cultural, linguistic and artistic identity'.

[1] The Constitution of the Republic of Angola was approved in 2010 and published in Diário Da República 1 Series nº 23 from 5 February 2010. http://www.tribunalconstitucional.ao/uploads/%7B9555c635-8d7c-4ea1-b7f9-0cd33d08ea40%7D.pdf Access August 19, 2014.

'The State shall promote and encourage the preservation and enhancement of historic, cultural and artistic heritage of the Angolan people'.

In this perspective of effective integration of the culture in development policies that the Angolan Government has since January 11, 2011 approved by Presidential Decree n° 15/11, its Cultural Policy for a period of 10 years.[2] This policy recognizes culture as a significant component, with immediate effects on the internal cohesion of the Angolan society, aiming to build a united, developed and prosperous nation.

The Angolan culture, as described in this policy, has a rich cultural and natural heritage composed of a diversity of museum objects, monuments, historical and archaeological sites, cultural landscapes, historic buildings and centers, etc., including the variety of intangible heritage.

The values of this cultural wealth must be preserved, studied and promoted within and outside of the country in order to be part of the key strategic challenges which aim the progress, development and affirmation of the country worldwide.

This cultural policy recognizes the cultural heritage (museums, monuments and cultural sites, including archaeological heritage) as one of the pillars of the cultural development of Angola. On this basis, the Government and civil society have a duty to promote and support all efforts aimed at the preservation, enhancement and management of these properties. It is the government's responsibility through the Ministry of Culture, to define the conditions and criteria for classification of monuments and sites on the national heritage list.

It is on this basis that the State has funded throughout this period the Angolan heritage policies in order, not only to safeguard the still existing heritage, but also to make it accessible to the Angolan people in allowing him to participate in the efforts of the national reconstruction.

Law of Cultural Heritage

In order to make more effective the implementation of the Angolan cultural policy strategy in the field of heritage, the Government approved, in 2005, the Law of Cultural Heritage[3] to make clearer the conditions and criteria for the conservation and enhancement of the national cultural heritage.

Before analyzing what is described in this law, it is important to make a little detour into the past to see how Angola, as a young nation, is expected, just after its independence, to face the challenges of safeguarding and promoting its rich heritage.

Decree 80/76

From 1976 until 2005, public policies on the safeguarding, protection and enhancement of the Angolan cultural heritage were governed by Decree 80/76 of September, 3rd.[4]

Having a look to the context in which this decree was prepared, it does not address explicitly the issue related to the overall management of the Angolan cultural heritage. It emphasizes more the operations of preserving and protecting the heritage in insisting on the return of the Angolan heritage illegally subtracted from the Angolan people.

Regarding the safeguarding of the Angolan cultural heritage, the decree implicitly addresses the issue of the heritage management touching on the importance of the Angolan people access to their culture, as the basis of national reconstruction through the cultural heritage.

[2] The Angolan Cultural Policy was approved in 2011 and published in Diário Da República 1 Series nº 6 from 11 January 2011.

[3] The Law of Cultural Heritage was approved in 2005 and published in Diário Da República 1 Series 120 from 7 October 2010.

[4] The Decree 80/76 was approved in 1976 and published in Diário Da República 1 Series nº 244 from 14 October 1976.

Among the properties considered as historical and cultural heritage, the decree makes some notes, in its Article 1, on the archeological heritage, especially the collections that deserve special protection because of their vulnerability to the illicit trafficking:

Article 1:

Are considered as historic documents:

- 'Archeological and Paleontological collections which have been classified';
- 'Buildings, sites, objects with special character, statues, bridges, other constructions which have been classified'.

Law of Cultural Heritage (14/05):

Contrary to Decree 80/76, the Cultural Heritage Law approved in 2005, largely addresses issues of the safeguarding, protection, enhancement, promotion and dissemination of the Angolan cultural heritage involving the participation of all (decision makers, civil society, local communities, public in general).

This Law responds to the principles contained in the Constitution and Cultural Policy of the Republic of Angola. Thus, in its first article on the fundamental principles, the Law emphasizes the issue of access to culture via the use of cultural heritage for the construction of the national identity:

Article 1:

'This Law establishes the foundations of the political regime of the protection and enhancement of Cultural Heritage considered of special interest for understanding, maintaining and building the Angolan cultural identity'.

'The Policies of Cultural Heritage integrate the actions promoted by the State, provincial governments, local administrations, associations and sensitivities of civil society, to ensure in the national space, the realization of the right to culture and the cultural enjoyment in the various fields of social life'.

In its Article 4, the Law emphasizes the importance of a participatory management for better protection and enhancement of the national cultural heritage:

Article 4:

'The State, through the Ministry of trusteeship, Provincial Governments and Local Government should seek to promote awareness and citizen participation in the safeguarding of cultural heritage and ensure the conditions for their enjoyment'.

'Populations should be associated with the measures of protection and conservation and requested to collaborate in dignity, defense and enjoyment of Cultural Heritage'.

Contrary to Decree 80/76, the Law of cultural heritage has an entire section (Section IV) which clarifies the procedures and rules to be respected for the better management of the movable and unmovable archaeological property, by already defining what is meant by archaeological work.

Article 33:

'For the purposes of this law, the term 'archaeological work' stands for: all investigations whose purpose is the discovery of archaeological character goods, if these investigations involve excavation of soil or a systematic exploration of its surface, as in the case to perform in bed or subsoil of inland or territorial waters'.

Article 34:

'The completion of archaeological work on classified monuments, complexes and sites or in the process of classification, in their respective areas of protection and still in the unclassified buildings with an archaeological interest, requires prior authorization from the Ministry of trusteeship'.

Article 36:

'Anywhere where they assume the existence of monuments, ensembles or archaeological sites can be established by the Ministry of Trusteeship, with preventive and temporary character, an archaeological area of protection, to ensure the implementation of emergency work, with aims to determine their interest'.

Decree 53/13 of the Unmovable Heritage

Taking into account the various violations observed in applying the Law of Cultural Heritage due to the economic growth of Angola which is having a negative impact on the preservation of the heritage building, including some archaeological sites, the Angolan government through the Ministry of Culture strengthened measures for protecting the cultural properties with particular emphasis on the built heritage, in approving in 2013, the legislation on the unmovable heritage[5] which clearly determinates today the different categories of the heritage, the criteria and mechanisms of its inventory and classification (declassification) on the heritage national list.

In the spirit of this decree, the unmovable archaeological heritage is part of sites as defined in Article 3:

'Man or nature joint works, characteristic and homogeneous spaces which can be geographically limited, notable for its historical, archaeological, artistic, scientific or social interest.'

Besides clarifying the procedures of the inventory, classification and declassification of the built heritage, the decree makes little mention to the practical archaeological heritage management, except in its Article 39 that addresses the issue of funding for the management of unmovable heritage in danger:

Article 39:

'The expenses relating to the safeguarding of endangered cultural heritage by the execution of works in the public sector, including preliminary archaeological work, are supported by the promoters of the project, which must, for this purpose, include them in his budget'.

Current archaeological heritage management (conservation, promotion and archaeological research) follows the standards that are defined in the Law of Cultural Heritage, and practically, to those of the implementing decree on the unmovable heritage.

Despite the great efforts that have been made in the legal field for the past decade, the analysis of the current legislation shows that there is still a gap in the specific field of archaeological heritage management. Contrary to public policy for the protection of archaeological heritage of most states around the world, Angola has not developed a specific law or decree on this matter, which would reflect the principles described in charters (1990 ICOMOS Charter on archaeological Heritage Management) and other international conventions (UNESCO 2001 on the Protection of Underwater Heritage Convention, 1982 United Nations law of the Sea, etc.). These international legal instruments encourage the implementation of integrated conservation policies, programs, specialized training strategies and international cooperation.

[5] The legal instrument related to the Unnovable heritage was approved in 2013 and published under the Presidential Decree nº 53/13 pf June 6th in the Diário Da República 1 Series nº 106 from June 2013.

Another legal gap on the international protection of the archaeological heritage remains so far the non-ratification by the Angolan government of the 2001 UNESCO Convention on the Underwater Cultural Heritage, which encourages States to develop bilateral, regional and cooperation, especially considering the wide side of the Atlantic ocean Angola shares since centuries with some African countries and which is explored by several multinational companies to avoid intensifying unauthorized commercial exploitation of underwater heritage, including naturally archaeological heritage.

Institutional Framework

The institutionalization of public policies in the field of heritage began in 1976 with the publication of the Decree 80/76. It is through this legal provision that the Angolan Government established in 1976, the National Commission of Museums in the Ministry of Education and Culture. According to Article 1 of the decree, the institution was responsible for: 'Inventory, classify, conserve move, restore and determine the conditions of use of all elements of the Historic Cultural Heritage of the Angolan People'.

Later, the National Commission of Museums has evolved into the National Department of Museums and Monuments of the National Council of Culture. In 1988, with the birth of the State Secretariat of Culture, the former department has evolved to embody the National Institute of Cultural Heritage (INPC) that, until 2009, covered the following areas: unmovable heritage, movable heritage (museums) and intangible heritage. Since 2009, the museums are under the supervision of the National Directorate of Museums (DINAM) of the Ministry of Culture. This directorate also oversees the National Archaeological Museum of Benguela (MNAB).

If we talk about the specific management of archaeological heritage, both institutions are responsible for:

- On one side, the INPC, the body currently under the Ministry of Culture, manages the inventory, documentation, classification, identification of all the monuments and sites of the country closely with provincial directorates of culture according to its missions and as stated in the Article 35 of the Decree on the unmovable heritage, which states:

'The National Institute of Cultural Heritage is responsible for preparing instruments which ensure the overall management of unmovable cultural heritage and their values of homogeneity, authenticity, integrity and uniqueness.'

- On the other side, the National Museum of Archaeology, under the DINAM, also manages the Archaeological Heritage (collections and sites), according to its missions which are: 'Investigate, collect, identify, classify, preserve, exhibit and disseminate the historical-cultural, archaeological, geological, anthropological, numismatic, literature heritage and other ...'. Faced with this management at double speed, there is no ambiguity in considering that the limits in the missions of the two institutions are not clearly defined? For an effective management of the national archaeological heritage, the National Archaeological Museum of Benguela, should it not act as an advisory body to the INPC, which should also include in its structure a specific technical department of Archaeology? Or should there be in the Ministry of Culture an autonomous directorate responsible for preparing policies and programs able to effectively meet the needs of archaeological heritage management, especially when we consider the management gaps and role conflicts observed at INPC and MNAB.

Management of Archeological Heritage: Actions and Perspectives

Despite the inadequacy observed today in public management policies of archeological heritage, some activities have been implemented to improve the current framework:

Inventory and documentation

Under the colonial legislation (not repealed after the independence regarding classified moments and sites), the Decree 80/76, the current law on heritage and its decree on the unmovable heritage and other legal requirements (law of town planning, land law, etc.), the Ministry of Culture, through the INPC, classified today about 22 archaeological sites, especially in southern region of Angola (Provinces of Benguela, Kwanza Sul and Namibe) and whose the most symbolic are the rock art sites of Tchitundu-Hulu and Ebo.

Apart from classified archaeological sites, there is an archeological collection estimated to about 9000 objects preserved in the National Archaeology Museum of Benguela coming from different archaeological sites of Benguela (Tchitono, Ekapi, Cimo, Pima, Moçambes, Ponta da Vaca, Dungo, Cachama, etc.). The collection is largely composed of lithic objects, ceramics, wooden objects, bone objects, coins including the bone remains of the mammal skeleton discovered on the site Dungo V.

There is also another archaeological collection at the Regional Museum of Dundo, which is the result of geological research in the eastern region of Angola and a part is now in the collection of MNAB.

Training and Research

Regarding the issue of training in Archaeology, neither of the two institutions (INPC, MNAB) has highly trained technicians. The Angolan archaeologists' core is formed by:

- 2 Doctors in Archaeology trained at the University of Paris 1 Panthéon-Sorbonne and the University of Toulouse (France);
- 2 PhD students to graduate in Archaeology at the University of Paris 1 and University of Trás-os-Montes and Alto Douro in Portugal and 1 MA student in Archaeology at the Polytechnic Institute of Tomar in Portugal.

A core of five technicians to develop Archaeology research in all the country, rich in archaeological heritage, seems to be insignificant considering the elapsed time since the public management policies of cultural heritage were institutionalized and the Angolan archaeological wealth which has to be preserved and promoted.

Apart from small training initiatives in Archaeology developed at University Katyavala Buila of Benguela, no Angolan university has a discipline dedicated mainly to Archaeology that could bridge this gap, and neither has prospects to open this discipline in the short term.

The only consolidated strategies today in the field of training and archaeological research are implemented in partnership with European universities and research centers such as the Franco-Angolan program in Archaeology.

Field School of Baia-Farta in Benguela

The Field School in Baia Farta in Benguela Province emerges as a product of the Franco-Angolan cooperation in the field of Archaeology, supported by the French Embassy in Angola. This cooperation dates back to the 1990s and has contributed much in advance of Angolan archaeological research, either in the training of high-level technicians as already mentioned, either in the work field that lead to excavations and consequently to the enrichment of the collection of the National Archaeological Museum. This cooperation is annually carried out by a Team of Researchers in African Archaeology from the University of Paris 1 – Panthéon Sorbonne, by the staff of the National Archaeological Museum of Benguela and some lecturers and students from the University of Katyavala Buila.

Over the years, there was a need to connect theory to practice creating the Field School of Baia Farta whose aim is to familiarize the technicians from the National Museum of Archaeology and students

FIGURE 1. FIELD WORK AT DUNGO IV SITE (BENGUELA) DURING THE 2014 FIELD SCHOOL.
© MANUEL GUTIERREZ, UNIVERSITY OF PARIS 1

in history from the University of Katyavala Buila to methods of archaeological excavations, the identification of archaeological objects and the recognition of stratigraphic levels, data recording and handling of discovered objects.

With few resources, especially from the Angolan side which should ensure logistical conditions and some support materials for the transportation of objects, this experience has produced great results to enrich the museum collection and to improve the preservation and enhancement of the archaeological heritage of the region, in addition to train students who may become future Museum technicians and to create vocations for a career in Archaeology (figure 1). Some of the discovered materials are dated to determine its chronology.

Within this Franco-Angolan cooperation was possible to make the dating of the remains from the same stratigraphic level where the remains of the whale skeleton were found at the site of Dungo V, estimated 350,000 years and the lithic materials buried underground on site Dungo IV estimated 2 million years. With these recent data, the site of Dungo IV can be considered as the oldest archeological site of Angola and that part of the African continent (Gutierrez 2013).

Other Programs of Archeological Research

Archeological Excavations in Mbanza Kongo

Since 2006, the Ministry of Culture of Angola through the National Institute of Cultural Heritage is preparing the nomination of the Historic City of Mbanza Kongo, classified as a national heritage in

June 2013, on the World Heritage List of UNESCO. Given its archaeological potential, the Historic Centre of Mbanza Kongo, is also declared as an archaeological area, in accordance with Article 36 of the Law of Cultural Heritage.

One of the criteria of Outstanding Universal Value should justify that Mbanza Kongo is one of the most important cities and one of the oldest cities in Sub-Saharan Africa which was created in XIII Centuries by Nimi The Lukeni. It was the economic capital of the Kingdom of Kongo in the precolonial era that influenced the kingdoms of the sub-region (Kakongo, Ngoyo and Loango) and the development of the city had a close connection with the period of the Iron Age. The key issue is to archaeologically demonstrate these trade relations between the Kingdom of Kongo and kingdoms mentioned above.

To collect convincing evidence materials on the role and the historical influence of the Kingdom of Kongo on the rest of the kingdoms, appropriate conditions have been created for the systematic archaeological excavations to develop shortly, as indispensable sources in confirming the historical information available.

This excavations program started in 2011 in the framework of cooperation between the National Institute of Cultural Heritage and the University of Yaoundé (Cameroon), the University of Coimbra (Portugal), The University of Brussels (Belgium) and UNESCO.

In the process of implementing this program, several campaigns of excavations were and continue to be held in Mbanza Kongo during which remains of ceramics were found and among of them, some of the style from Central Africa developed through the phenomenon of the Iron Age pits and which date between XIV and XVI centuries, the period of first contact with Europeans. Apart from the pottery, other remains were found: human remains, metal objects, coals, foundations of one of the old buildings whose original function has not been defined (Assombang, Mbida & Lopes, 2014).

Tchitundu-Hulu Project

In the process of the nomination of the archaeological complex of Tchitundu-Hulu on the World Heritage List, the Ministry of Culture through the National Institute of Cultural Heritage carried out, in March of 2011, in partnership with the African World Heritage Fund (AWHF), based in South Africa, an international workshop on the development of the management plan for the archaeological site of Tchitundu-Hulu.

Apart from the transmission and application of principles for the development of a management plan, this workshop aimed to identify emergency conservation measures for the site with purpose to prepare, in the future, its risk management plan.

The workshop was facilitated by a team of specialists from the University Eduardo Mondlane in Mozambique, the University of Witwatersrand in South Africa, the Ministry of Culture of Cabo Verde, TARA (Trust for African Rock Art) and the African World Heritage Fund. The audience included forty heritage professionals whose thirty-five from the INPC, the Provincial Directorates of Culture and local communities of Angola, including the current traditional ruler of the community of Tchitundu Hulu (which served as a guide during the field visit) and five participants from Portuguese and Spanish-speaking countries in Africa (São Tome and Principe and Equatorial Guinea). Based on an interactive methodology, this workshop had discussed issues relating to the implementation of the guidelines of the World Heritage Convention, the stakes of the global strategy to achieve a balanced representation of sites on the World Heritage List, the techniques for the development of a management plan, including site assessment by the SWOT (Strength, Weakness, Opportunities, Threat) analysis. These discussions were complemented by the analysis of the management models of some rock art sites from South Africa and Malawi and a field visit in the site of Tchitundu-Hulu. As results, apart from the building capacity of about 30 Angolan heritage professionals on the development of a management plan, several recommendations were made by the trainers and participants who constitute the very basis of the nomination project of Tchitundu- Hulu on the World Heritage List. Among these, we can mention:

- The determination of the site boundaries: the core area and the buffer zone taking into account the desert of Namibe and the focus area of the Welwitchia mirabilis plant;
- The completion of a deep survey and research on the state of conservation of paintings and engravings;
- The development of an anthropological study of traditional practices of local people to enhance the spiritual dimension of the site environment;
- The development of a management plan based on a participatory approach involving all stakeholders;
- The identification of opportunities for specific training in the field of the archaeological heritage management in order to strengthen the management of the various rock art sites on the Angolan territory.

Archeological Research Project in Ebo

In the framework of implementing the project for the preservation and enhancement of rock paintings of the Ebo (Province of Kwanza Sul) (figure 2), a partnership has been built between the National Institute of Cultural Heritage, the National Archaeological Museum of Benguela and the Polytechnic Institute of Tomar (Portugal).

FIGURE 2. ROCK PAINTINGS FROM THE SITE OF NDALAMBIRI IN EBO (KWANZA SUL).
© ZIVA DOMINGOS

One of the actions developed up to now is the preparation of a thesis on the rock art sites of Ebo whose last field mission conducted in 2013 allowed to collect some samples of pigments from the site of Ndalambiri, classified as a national heritage in 1974. These pigments were analyzed by Micro-Raman Spectroscopy at the Laboratory of Physics and Earth Sciences (University of Ferrara, Italy) in the framework of this partnership. The results of this analysis show the existence of coal in the black pigment, of hematite and quartz in red pigment and calcite in white pigment (Martins *et al.*, 2014). The dating performed on the black pigment of the later layer paintings report the transition to the XVIII Century (Oosterbeek, 2013) and mark a new stage in the archeological research on the rock art of Angola whose first analysis on C14 were performed on the pigments from the site of Tchitundu-Hulu (Province of Namibe) pointing to an approximate date of 2,500 years (2596 ± 53 BP) (Gutierrez, 1996).

Conclusion

Despite about 40 years of independence, the development of Angola was blocked for nearly two decades because of the civil war. Since the end of the tragedy in 2002, it is noticed today an awareness of heritage issues from both policy makers and the population and an investment from the government in the field of culture with a growth in the budget for the social sector. Notwithstanding all efforts made by the institutions in charge of the archaeological heritage, they still continue to face several challenges that open up prospects cooperation at the national and international level. The critical analysis of the current archaeological heritage management shows that the following strategies should continue to be implemented:

- The development of appropriate legislation of the archeological heritage management which takes into account the issues related to the preventive Archaeology, the underwater Archaeology and the Archaeology of contract; While waiting for the future legal instrument, actions of sensitization and dissemination must continue to make the current legislation (Heritage Law and Decree on the Unmovable Heritage) more effective;
- The development of clear missions for the existing management bodies and the establishment of local bodies (local museums of Archaeology) to meet the challenges of planning and development program while preserving the rich national archaeological heritage as part of the heritage of humanity along with the local communities;
- The capacity building of heritage professionals with achieving technical and academic training in Archaeology to lead, in the medium term, to the opening of an Archaeology department at the UAN or the UKB, not talking right now of a faculty of history and Archaeology.
- The development of archaeological research projects involving national researchers and professionals and local communities in order to improve the quality of life of these holders and guardians of this heritage.
- As stressed by Yambo (2009), these challenges can only be met with the help of international cooperation. Therefore, partnerships above mentioned and others which will certainly emerge, should be strengthened and work within a framework of transparence and equality that encourages the exchange and sharing of information on the results produced by research projects.

References

Assombang, R.; Mbinda, C.; Lopes, M. C. (2014) – *Mbanza Kongo: Mission archéologique. Rapport: janvier-février 2014.* Paris: UNESCO. 30 p.

Gutierrez, M. (2013) – Angola, la découverte d'une préhistoire. *Archéologia.* N.°506: janvier 2013. Dijon: les Éditions Faton. p. 62-67.

Gutierrez, M. (1996) – *L'art pariétal de l'Angola.* Paris: L'Harmattan. 320 p.

Martins, C. P.; Rosina, P.; Gomes, H.; Holakooei, P.; Benjamim, M. H.; Valongo, P.; Domingos, Z.; Oosterbeek, L. (2014) – Análise de pigmentos das pinturas rupestre do Abrigo Dalambiri

(Ebo): um novo passo na investigação arqueológica em Angola. In *Arqueologia Ibero-Americana e Transatlântica: Arqueologia, Sociedade e Território.* Erechim: Habilis press. p. 129-145.

Oosterbeek, L. (2013) – *Ebo: Mapeamento e registo de arte Rupestre da Zona Centro-Oeste de Angola.* Relatório Final. Tomar: Instituto Politécnico de Tomar. 126 p.

Yambo, F. X. (2009) – Préface. *Art rupestre en Angola, Province de Namibe.* Saint-Maur-des-Fossés: Sépia. p. 8-9.

The Legal Protection of Archaeological Heritage in Mozambique (1994-2014)

Solange L. Macamo
Archaeologist (PhD), National Director for Cultural Heritage,
Ministry of Culture and Eduardo Mondlane University Lecturer
solangemacamo@gmail.com

Leonardo Adamowicz
Archaeologist (M.A.) & Anthropologist (PhD), President of ICOMOS-Mozambique,
Eduardo Mondlane University and the Polytechnic University Lecturer
leonardo.adamowicz@gmail.com

Abstract

This paper discusses the importance of the legal protection of archaeological heritage in Mozambique, by accessing the results achieved in the past 20 years. Clearly, the legislation itself is not enough to protect heritage. This should go side by side with the establishment of a Management System (MS), not only for archaeology but for the whole cultural heritage. Initially the paper was presented by the first author during the XVII World UISPP Congress- International Union of Pre-historic and Proto-Historic Sciences in Burgos, Spain. Later on, the second author accepted to join to it in order to give his valuable contribution, considering his collaborative role in the process of the protection of archaeological heritage in Mozambique.

Keywords

Mozambique, protective measures, archaeological heritage, research permit, sustainable conservation

Résumé

Cet article traite de l'importance de la protection juridique du patrimoine archéologique au Mozambique, en accédant à des résultats obtenus au cours des 20 dernières années. De toute évidence, la loi elle-même n'est pas assez pour protéger le patrimoine. Cela devrait aller côte à côte avec la mise en place d'un Système de Gestion (MS), non seulement pour l'archéologie, mais aussi pour le patrimoine culturel ensemble. Initialement le document a été présenté par le premier auteur pendant de XVII UISPP Congrès Mondial – Union Internacional des Sciences Préhistoriques et Protohistoriques de Burgos, Espagne. Plus tard, le second auteur accepté à se joindre afin de donner sa précieuse contribution, étant donné son rôle de collaboration dans le processus de la protection du patrimoine archéologique au Mozambique.

Mots-clés

Mozambique, mesures de protection, patrimoine archéologique, permis de recherche, conservation durable

Introduction

The growing interest of the archaeological heritage in Mozambique is indicated by the recent opening of a course of Archaeology and heritage management attached to the Department of Archaeology and Anthropology (DAA), in the Faculty of Arts and Social Sciences of Eduardo Mondlane University. In the Ministry of Culture, a MS for heritage is being reflected by its National Directorate for Cultural Heritage (D.N.P.C.) with the support of the National Board for Cultural Heritage (C.N.P.C.). The objective of this is to help to better protect the recovered archaeological finds and the excavated sites (Map 1), for the promotion of heritage education and cultural tourism (c.f. Filipe 2009, pp: 90-100; Muocha 2014, 59-66; as a contribution to development programs.

This paper will access the legal status of archaeological heritage in Mozambique, since from 1994, when the regulation for the protection of the archaeological heritage was adopted (Decree 27/94).[1]

[1] Decree Nr. 27/94 20 of June, Regulation for the Protection of the Archaeological Heritage. Maputo: Republic Bulletin, official publication of the Republic of Mozambique.

MAP 1. SOUTHERN MOZAMBIQUE, SHOWING THE PRINCIPAL ARCHAEOLOGICAL SITES MENTIONED IN THE TEXT (© L. ADAMOWICZ)

Since that period, there have been specific principles and norms for carrying out archaeological work on national territory. The experiences resulting from its implementation will be here remarked.

Clearly, the legislation itself is not enough to stop damages to the archaeological sites. Some of the problems are related to the abandonment of sites, due to absence of site managers and lack of resources (Macamo 1996, pp. 813-4). Another concern is the challenge related to development programs, in the context of the protection of the whole cultural heritage.

The discussion departs from the archaeological sites across the country and from our personal observations, during the working process. However, we have chosen to illustrate the example of the Zimbabwe Tradition site of Manyikeni (XIII-XVII century), were management systems were implemented (Sinclair 1987, 99; Macamo 2006, 213-230; 2011a, 310-342). Generally, this Tradition is characterized by the presence of a geometric design and graphite-burnished pottery (Macamo 2006, 63 *apud* Pwiti 1990, 204). A distinct dual settlement pattern divided into an area for the elite living inside the walling and an outside area for the commoners is also present, as studied in Manyikeni (Morais and Sinclair 1980). The protected Matola site is related to the Early Farming Communities in Southern Mozambique, being associated to the Bantu speaking population expansion (Cruz e Silva 1976; Morais 1988, 90-98). It is an example were development programs are taking place and it is compared to the similar site of Eduardo Mondlane University Campus in Maputo (Sinclair *et al.* 1987, Morais 1988, 85-90). Both sites share a similar Matola Tradition because of the pottery design with typical incised decoration motifs. The Massingir cluster of sites is shown as an example of heritage under the impact of population settlement, due to their proximity to the Kruger Park. The sites constitute an evidence of the transition period from the first to second millennium AD. The concentration of animal bone remains there is an indication of the importance of cattle herding economy at the time (Duarte 1988, 60-61; Macamo & Risberg 2007; Macamo 2011b, 24-27; Macamo & Machava 2011). The osteological sample indicates that in Massingir there were even more species (Morais 1988, 118).

We shall first present the archaeological context and then outline the legal protection history. The content of the protective legislation is also summarized. This is followed by an analysis of the general context in which the responsible preservation institution deals with the whole heritage. This includes the State role, through its cultural sector and particularly the D.N.P.C. The collaborative role of the University DAA, in this process is emphasized. We also show how the legislation is implemented; using the above mentioned selected sites for this work. Lastly, a general discussion on the heritage management system is made.

The archaeological context and heritage management projects

After Independence, between 1975 and 1980, there were about 7 archaeologists in Mozambique. We are taking the risk to mention the contribution of the following people, without willing to exclude any body that might have been involved in this process and that is not mentioned by mistake. J. Morais together with R. Duarte, M. L. Dias, T. Cruz e Silva and J. S. Martinez were the founder of the archaeology section that was initially under the directorship of Prof. G. Soares de Carvalho. Later on, J. Stephen from Southampton University, as well as P. Sinclair from Cambridge University, L. Adamowicz from the University of Warsaw were also attached to the section (Morais 1988, 47). Thanks to their contribution archaeological research areas were clearly defined in the country. There were also other researchers interested in archaeology whose contribution was important for the development of archaeology in Mozambique. Some of them, however, have left archaeology, but their contribution is still recognized.

Archaeological research activities were carried out at DAA, created in 1980 and incorporated into the former Faculty of Arts of Eduardo Mondlane University (Duarte 1988, 69, Morais 1988, 47). Between 1982 and 1985 four Swedish assistants were appointed to the Department by the Swedish Central Board of Antiquities, being P.I. Lindqvist, L. Jonsson, Nils-Gustaf Nydolf and Gunilla Wickman-Nydolf (Sinclair *et al.*, 1987; Morais, 1988, 48).

Archaeologists also combined their research efforts with museum conservation, on the basis of collaborative work with the former National Service of Museums and Antiquities whose director was Ricardo T. Duarte. This helped to establish the open-air museum of Manyikeni in 1977 (Sinclair 1987, 99); the first interpretive center created in the country.

Thanks to the contribution of international cooperation, initially with SIDA/SAREC (Swedish Agency for Research Cooperation) and the British Institute in East Africa, archaeological research projects with a training component have increased. This also was combined with legal protective measures, to help to preserve the sites and disseminate knowledge, the example of which is Manyikeni. The other example is 'CIPRIANA' (campaign for the implementation of the archaeological research project in Nampula province) founded by L. Adamowicz (Adamowicz 1987, 47-144). This project developed a Circle of Interest in Archaeology, an interesting experience, which helped greatly to disseminate archaeology and heritage education among young people.

From late 1990 to 2004 two major archaeological heritage projects operated in the country operated, within a regional framework, in cooperation with SIDA-SAREC: UOFU-Urban Origin Project and

HRAC-Human Responses to Environmental Change and in Africa and Sri Lanka (Sinclair 1995, 1997, 1999, 57-62; Macamo and Ekblom 2005, 125-138). Professor P. Sinclair was the scientific coordinator of the projects and he worked with national country coordinators. The projects were implemented in Vilankulo district, in Manyikeni and Chibuene, a coastal trading station from the late first and early second millennium AD (Sinclair 1982, 1987, 86-90). Two community heritage management committees were established in Vilankulo, to help to protect the sites.

During the past 10 years, other major cooperation projects have helped significantly to train archaeologists in Mozambique, combining both research activities with heritage management:

- Archaeological and Cultural Project, funded by the University of Calgary, Canada, directed by Julio Mercader;
- Archaeological Research and Cultural Heritage Management Project, funded by Norway, directed by Tore Saetersdal from the University of Bergen.

In 2010 the University course in Archaeology and Heritage Management initiated in Mozambique, under the DAA. The course was directed by the department fellows, first Albino Jopela followed by Katia Filipe.

This training course has now been strengthened with the interchange international teaching programs, namely with Uppsala University, Sweden, under the Linnaeus-Palme program, whose local coordinator is Anneli Ekblom. Also, the investment projects such as Vale Mozambique LDA (Brazilian Multinational) offer promise given the opportunities to employ young archaeologists in the protection of sites in danger, through the implementation of rescue archaeological protective measures determined under the Regulation (*Decree 27/94*).

Hopefully, the number of archaeologists in Mozambique soon might increase significantly up to 30 people.

The development of the protective legislation

In pre-colonial time, local people respected their archaeological heritage, mainly sites with visible structures, because they believed that they are associated to their ancestors. This is related mainly to the Zimbabwe Tradition and rock art sites (Macamo and Saetersdal 2004, pp. 193-8). Local people do so even to date, with an active involvement of the community leaders (c.f. Ndoro 2001; Jopela 2014). The recognition of socio cultural values by local communities attached to archaeological sites help to protect heritage. This is also the reason why the archaeological sites remained preserved for such a long time and we are able now to research them.

Legal protective measures for the archaeological heritage in Mozambique were taken in the colonial times. In 1947, the former colonial Commission of Monuments did an important survey work of archaeological sites in Mozambique and established their inventory. Some of the sites were declared and published in the colonial Mozambique Official Bulletin. The example was Manyikeni, however, declared on the basis that it was a trade station of Great Zimbabwe that was Lusitanian (Portuguese).

After Independence, the Law for the Protection of Cultural Heritage (Law nr.10/1988)[2] was adopted but a specific Regulation for the protection of archaeological heritage was only made possible 20 years ago. The implementation of this legislation is made by the Ministry of Culture, through D.N.P.C., considered by Law, as competent authority. There are two departments in the D.N.P.C: department of museums and department of monuments that constitute an operational tool for the coordination of activities in the areas of movable and immovable heritage, respectively. This includes

[2] Law 10/88 from 22 December, about the Protection of Cultural Heritage. Maputo: Republic Bulletin, official publication of the Republic of Mozambique.

the implementation of the protective legislation. The main heritage management institutions are the museums (mainly the national ones, in the south and northern part of Mozambique) and the newly created Conservation Office for Mozambique Island, UNESCO World Heritage site, since 1991 (Macamo (Coord.) 2014).

With the publication of the Regulation (*Decree nr. 27/94*) and the appointment with due effect of the above mentioned National Board of Cultural Heritage a legal space was also cleared to applicants for underwater research programs on Mozambique's territorial waters to be made and evaluated. In fact, the C.N.P.C. is the main advising body composed of representatives from relevant ministries and government institutions, or even independent experts (mainly in the areas of arts, archaeology, architecture, history, anthropology). Its advising role to the Minister helps him to take decisions related to the use of heritage both tangible and intangible (mainly heritage attached to historical buildings, archaeological sites, Mozambique Island). The decisions weather a site or property should be classified or not is made after an advice of this board. The board also assists in drafting specific regulations that are still missing for the implementation of the Law, aiming to ensure the establishment and development of a MS for the heritage.

To add to this, in 2010 two complementary policies were approved by the Cabinet Meeting: the Museum Policy[3] and the Monument Policy.[4] For example, the definition of the management museum policy for the objects is applied to archaeology too. At the same time, the Monument Policy defines archaeological monuments and elements as the first priority area of intervention.

According to the Law Nr. 10/88, 22nd December:

'Any archaeological works or the opening of caves, grottos and geological formations for the purpose of carrying out anthropological or paleontological research is subject to prior authorisation by the relevant authorities'.

(Article Nr. 13)

'(...) Excavation works shall be carried out in accordance with the national and internationally valid principles and scientific norms'.

(Article Nr. 14)

The Decree 27/94 gives more details concerning the protection of the archaeological heritage. These include' all archaeological elements which under *Law Nr. 10/88, 22 December* are regarded as classified property of the cultural heritage, including the buffer zone and access routes where are clear signs of remains of movable and immovable property or any other remain of human existence identified or that may come to be identified on the ground, underground, on riverbeds and under waters of the continental platform which shall be preserved *in situ* or pursuant to the provisions of these rules'.

The regulation sets out such rules as the following:

'It is forbidden to carry out archaeological excavations and surveys without a certifying license issued by the relevant authority (…)'.

'Authorization and issuing of licenses for archaeological works are the prerogative of the National Directorate for Cultural Heritage and museums and other public national bodies indicated by the Ministry of Culture which include in their working programs research and protection of the archaeological heritage'.

(Article 3)

[3] Resolution No. 11/2010 of 2nd of June, which approves the policy on monuments. Bulletin of the Republic No. 22 (I).

[4] Resolution No. 12/2010 of 2nd of June, which approves the policy on monuments. Bulletin of the Republic No. 22 (I).

The implementation of the protective legislation in Archaeology

There is a data base of the known archaeological sites in Mozambique. According to this there are: 27 Rock Art Sites, 87 Stone Age Sites, 371 Early Iron Age, 451 Late Iron Age settlements, 128 Sacred Places, 205 Historical Archaeology Sites and 7 Industrial Archaeology Sites (National Archaeological Database, records updated in December 2014). The data base which is the National Inventory of the Archaeological Sites is established at University. Hilário Madiquida, who is presently the Head Archaeology section, is responsible for it. The National Archaeological Computerization Program was initially created by L. Adamowicz (1988) in the DAA at Eduardo Mondlane University and developed by the International Council of Monuments and Sites (ICOMOS) – Mozambique with substantial cooperation of the UNESCO Commission in Mozambique.

Following the recorded sites, DAA is the Depository of the Archaeological Sites and is responsible in informing the Ministry of Culture about the state of conservation of sites, trough D.N.P.C. In fact, the two sectors coordinate efforts to preserve the sites. Likewise, permits for excavations are given by D.N.P.C. after DAA having had analyzed the proposed research projects by the applicants.

In the Ministry of Culture there is a Registration Book for archaeologists. Presently there are 26 archaeologists that were registered in this Book. It is in the basis of having been registered in the Ministry of Culture that archaeologists are given licenses for excavations. However, due to lack of specialized staff working in the area the procedures are not yet accurate.

During the past 20 years permits, corresponding to archaeological research activities in Mozambique were given to applicants by D.N.P.C. or by any other equivalent competent authority (see Table 1 in the end of the article). However, this will exclude underwater Archaeology because licenses were given under special contracts.

According to the Regulation archaeologists with a license should provide intermediate reports and a final report of the excavations. They should also publish their own scientific results of the excavations (*Article 5, Decree nr. 27/94*). Licenses for excavations are given for 3 years, but they can be renewed in accordance with specific rules.

Protective Measures

Local community support and effective protective policies are essential to ensure that the physical remains of its cultural legacy remain intact and are accessible to its people and tourists. Unfortunately, as every nation on the planet, Mozambique also faces the challenge posed by the tragic and continuing loss of cultural heritage sites to theft, vandalism, development, armed conflict and neglect.

Mozambican Government has taken some measures for the protection of archaeological heritage, on the basis of the above mentioned national laws, regarding site protection, having also ratified the *1972 UNESCO Convention for the Protection of World Cultural and Natural Heritage*. The government and megaproject such as SASOL, ANADARKO, RIO TINTO, VALE, etc. supports environmental impact assessment (EIA) with important cultural heritage and archaeological component (rescue survey, conservation and archaeological excavation projects) every year. Altogether, about seven museums have been established to house collections and there is more and more international cooperation on archaeological sites. However, it is also obvious that these measures are still far from sufficient for such a large country. Many problems have remained unsolved for a long time. Laws and international conventions if they are not properly implemented they will remain only paper constructs for many people and authorities. Heritage institutions are absent at local level for the daily monitoring of the whole cultural heritage. Most of the decisions and implementation of projects are taken at central level. Education and training regarding cultural heritage are very lacking and the local public attitude is somewhat indifferent. We think that the biggest problem is the absence of the MS for the whole heritage. The present Government structure for heritage management is inefficient and needs to be revised.

Some of the problems affecting the protection of the archaeological heritage:

- The Archaeological site of Eduardo Mondlane University is part of the Matola tradition, but this is not known by many people. There is a need to place an explanatory signboard.
- The Archaeological site of Matola has a signboard that helps to create awareness. At the moment, a private hotel is being built on this site, without the necessary care after the finds that may occur.
- The Massingir area yielded an important cluster of sites to be furthermore investigated. The sites are at risk of disappearance due to a population settlement program at the Limpopo Kruger Park.

The main objective of the National Directorate for Cultural Heritage is to increase public concern about our cultural heritage. This is the most needed step towards site protection in Mozambique. Heritage education that has been carried out through popular publications is still far to be satisfactory. What is needed mostly is the combination of effective efforts from the national, provincial and local levels.

We understand the importance of international cooperation and exchange for protection of our cultural heritage. And we know clearly what kinds of cooperation and exchange are necessary and effective in Mozambique. So, we are very pleased to offer the best professional advice on the protection of heritage sites. Actually, we have been quite successful in this area. We are sure that training and media are the most important factors for increasing public concern about cultural heritage protection. We have held some training activities for young people in the last two years. Recently, in 2014 we have published a manual for an effective conservation of immovable cultural heritage in Mozambique (Jopela, 2014).

Below follow some examples of protective measure applied in Mozambique:

- The involvement of local stakeholders appears to be the most efficient measure towards the protection and conservation of the whole heritage in Mozambique.
- Other accompanying measures comprise mainly museum interpretation.
- Display in small exhibitions of the excavated finds is an important protective measure and useful teaching tool, in the D.N.P.C. This also helps to attract more tourists. Students prepare them in the framework of their training.

However, signboards are the most visible and popular measures, being the most important ones (Muocha 2005). Signboards are found in roads and on the site. All of them display the relevant Mozambique Law for the Protection of Archaeological Heritage:

Road signboards

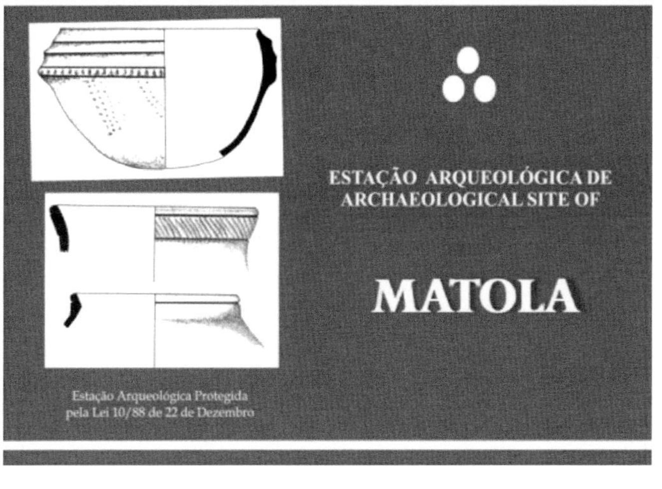

Figure 1. Matola, an early farming community site. The typical Matola pottery design can be seen

In situ protective signboards

FIGURE 2. PROTECTIVE SIGNBOARD AT MANYIKENI ZIMBABWE TRADITION SITE

Didactic signboards

FIGURE 3A-B. THE STONE ENCLOSURE OF CHIBUENE IS EXPLAINED FOR VISITORS AND FOR TEACHING PURPOSES (SINCLAIR 1987, 99) OF THE SITE. © S. MACAMO, 2014

Descriptive signboards

FIGURE 4. THE PRESENTATION OF CHIBUENE SITE

Reconstruction as a protective tool

Generally, we are protecting what we well know and what constitute some important value for us. The archaeological studies can help us substantially to know essential things about our cultural heritage and their historical value throughout three major goals: (1) chronology, (2) reconstruction, and (3) explanation. Chronologies establish the age of excavated materials. Reconstructions are models of what past human campsites, settlements, or cities – and their environments – might have looked like, and how they might have functioned. Explanations are scientific theories about what people living in the past thought and did.

Building on information about the chronology and composition of sites and their environments, archaeologists reconstruct how life might have looked in particular places at particular times. The reconstruction of past ways of life depends on interpretation of well-documented material remains and environmental remains in their chronological contexts.

In the 1975-78 British archaeologists P. Garlake (1976) and G. Barker (1978) preliminary reconstructed the *subsistence patterns* (ways of obtaining and producing food) of people who once lived in Manyikeni (Inhambane Province). In the 1980-84 Paul Sinclair (1987) refined Garlak's reconstructions analyzing the chemical composition of materials from Garlake and Barker studies and newly collected samples, including soil samples. The analyses not revealed any a shift in subsistence patterns over a 500-year period.

The reconstructions done by archaeologist use physical remains to create a picture of the past, explanations are attempts to answer questions about the past (figure 6). The reconstruction of changes in settlement and subsistence patterns of the inhabitants of the Cavala Industry of Late Stone Age and Nampula A Early Farming Communities in Nampula Province does not explain why these changes took place. They might be explained by any one factor or a combination of factors, such as iron using agriculture, Bantu communities' expansion, a dramatic change in weather patterns, an increase in the population, or a conscious decision to take advantage of a new discovery—agriculture. To be persuasive, an explanation has to fit with the existing archaeological data and stand up to scrutiny over time.

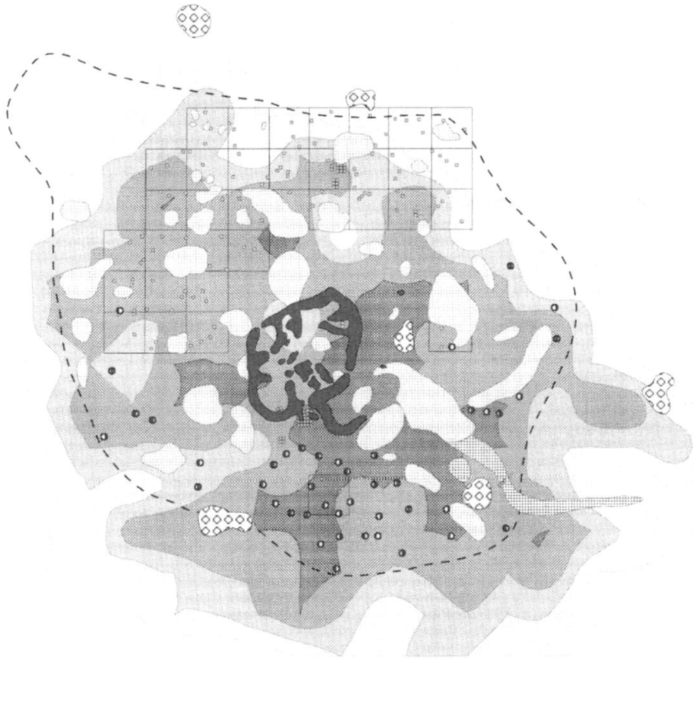

Figure 5. Sinclair's phosphate map with diachronic model of occupation reconstruction at Manyikeni (Sinclair *et al.* 1993, 2004)

Archaeologists may also try to recreate the artifacts and patterns they find in excavated sites in order to understand how artifacts were made and how patterns formed. In experimental archaeology, archaeologists perform controlled experiments to help interpret finds such as abandoned fire hearths, accumulations of waste from stone tool making, and collapsed buildings.

In Mozambique, we should still learn how archaeological study of large sites and other historical settlements involve both scientific excavation and conservation work. For example, at the capital of the sultanate Tungi ruins, in Cabo Delgado (northern Mozambique), archaeologist can excavate a temple and palace complex as well as large areas around the center. The excavators can also participate in mosque reconstruction and other collapsed structures. From ethnolinguistic sources, we already know that some buildings are mentioned in Palma Chronicles containing accounts of the rulers who ordered their construction. The excavations will provide archaeologists with new information about the ruling Swahili dynasties of Tungi. The accompanying conservation work will preserve the site for posterity and has created an attraction for tourism, a major part of the slave trade economy in northern Mozambique.

Present-day African societies can learn much from their predecessors. Applied archaeology refers to archaeological research that is designed to have practical and educational significance for modern societies. Since the late 1980s, archaeological research in in eastern and southern Africa concentrated some efforts to understand the dynamics of the processes leading to urbanization in Africa (Sinclair 1987, 22). A consideration of this factor was added to the already established recognition of the role, in the generation of towns and elites, of the control of local exchange networks and the injection into them of luxury goods derived from external trade (Sinclair, Shaw & Andah, 1993). The primary aim of these studies was to build up relative chronologies of cultural entities and promote conservation or reconstruction of some east African Swahili town and west African historical urban center in advanced degradation.

The Role of the Archaeologist

The role of the archaeologists is considered, in relation to the relevance of their work, not only when it comes to investigating sites, but mainly for their contribution in presenting solutions for the management of cultural heritage. This leads on the sustainable heritage conservation strategies. There are some questions arising from this reasoning: Firstly, to what extent the archaeological heritage can survive in face of development programs? Secondly, how relevant is the conservation of the archaeological heritage in the society, and how it can be valued?

The existing practice of rescue archaeology and its contribution to archaeological research is an answer in face of development programs. Here the role of archaeologist is relevant because of his

FIGURE 6. THE RESCUE ARCHAEOLOGICAL SURVEY IN CAPITAL OF THE SULTANATE TUNGI IN CABO DELGADO PENINSULA IN AREA FOR PROPOSED LIQUEFIED NATURAL GAS (LNG) PROJECT IN THE PALMA DISTRICT OF CABO DELGADO PROVINCE, NORTHERN MOZAMBIQUE (© L. ADAMOWICZ, 2011)

contribution to rescuing valuable archaeological sites. However, this legal solution is not always possible and certainly many sites will still remain unprotected. Some experiences resulting from dissemination work are important too, to make archaeology relevant in the country.

The contribution of cultural tourism is perceived for the satisfaction of community needs living near the sites and the necessary care to avoid its negative impact on the heritage (Macamo 2006, 222-9). Unfortunately, the use of sites for education and cultural tourism practice is not yet common, in Mozambique, even if there are some isolated initiatives. However, when it is properly planned, cultural tourism can help to solve the majority of heritage conservation problems and enable the implementation of the protective legal tools.

The archaeological heritage is a valuable resource like many others and it should be integrated in the development programs, trough management plans.

Education, tourism and sustainable conservation

The Mozambican policy in this point is well defined by Ministry of Education, Ministry of Tourism, Ministry of Cultures and their respective national and provincial agencies. Sustainable tourism, when done well, enhances education, supports local and regional cultures, alleviates poverty, empowers women, creates jobs, improves the wellbeing of local communities, and conserves natural resources. Understanding these transformative effects is mostly intuitive. For example, sustainable tourism development often showcases local culture and employs local people in doing so this alleviates poverty and increases the wellbeing of the community, which in turn creates revenue that can be reinvested in education. The association between sustainable tourism development and conservation, however, is indirect and less intuitive. More than anything else, the cultural agents, archaeologist and cultural anthropologist have realized that real change comes from understanding the culture and working with people to bridge the gap between what people espouse and what they do.

- The contribution of cultural tourism is meant to meet the needs of communities living near the sites and the necessary care to avoid its negative impact on the heritage (Mozambique Monument Policy).
- In spite of the Policy, the use of sites for education and cultural tourism practice is not yet common in Mozambique, even if there are some isolated initiatives.
- However, when it is properly planned, cultural tourism can help solve the majority of heritage conservation problems and enable the implementation of the protective legal tools.
- Archaeological heritage is a valuable resource like many others and it should be integrated in development programs, for its sustainable conservation.
- A MS is necessary for the cultural heritage in Mozambique, as discussed here, not only for sites and monuments, but also the oral traditions and the whole intangible cultural values. We hope to have contributed, in this paper, to achieve this goal.

References

Adamowicz, L. (1987) – Contribuição para o conhecimento da Arqueologia entre os rios Lúrio e Ligonha, Província de Nampula. Projecto CIPRIANA 1981/86. *Trabalhos de Arqueologia e Antropologia,* DAA/UEM, 3. 1987:45-144, Maputo.

Adamowicz, L. (1988b) – Contribuição para o registo computorizado das estações Arqueológicas em Moçambique. *Trabalhos de Arqueologia e Antropologia.* DAA/UEM. Maputo.

Adamowicz, L. (2011a) – *Relatório sobre a Prospecção Arqueológica de Salvaguarda, Barragem Moamba,* IMPACTO/Direcção Nacional das Águas.

Adamowicz, L. (2011b) – *Relatório sobre a Prospecção Arqueológica de Salvaguarda, Distrito do Mabote,* IMPACTO/SASOL.

Adamowicz, L. (2011c) – *Relatório sobre a Prospecção Arqueológica de Salvaguarda, Distrito do Palma (Penínsulas Afungi i Cabo Delgado),* IMPACTO/ANADARKO.

Barker, G. (1978) – Economic models for the Manekweni Zimbabwe, Mozambique. *Azania*13, 71-100.

Cruz e Silva, T. (1976) – *A preliminary report on an early iron age site: Matola IV/68.* Maputo: Instituto de Investigação Científica de Moçambique/Universidade Eduardo Mondlane.

Duarte, R. T. (1988) – Arqueologia da Idade do Ferro em Moçambique (1974 a 1988): Retrospectiva do trabalho realizado. *Trabalhos de Arqueologia e Antropologia* 5, 57-73.

Ekblom, E. & G. Lindsey (2010a) – Hierarchy and scale: testing the long-term role of water, grazing and nitrogen in the savanna landscape of Limpopo National Park (Mozambique). *Landscape Ecol* 25:1529-1546.

Ekblom, E. & G. Lindsey (2010b) – Fire history and fire ecology of Northern Kruger (KNP) and Limpopo National Park (PNL), southern Africa. *The Holocene* 20(7) 1063-1077.

Ekblom, E. & G. Lindsey (2010c) – Dung fungi as indicators of past herbivore abundance, Kruger and Limpopo National Park. Paleogeography, Paleoclimatology, *Paleoecology* 296: 14-27.

Ekblom, A., G. Lindsey & M. Notelid (2011) – A Historical Ecology of the Limpopo and Kruger National Parks and Lower Limpopo Valley. *Journal of Archaeology and Ancient History* 1: 3-29.

Filipe, K. C. (2009) – Community Based Cultural Heritage Management: A Stepping Stone Towards Sustainable Cultural Tourism. A Case Study of Vilanculos, Inhambane Province, Southern Mozambique. In: Gilbert Pwiti, Chantal. Radimilahy & Solange Macamo (Eds.), *Studies in the African Past* 7: 90-100.

Garlake, P. S. (1976) – An investigation of Manekweni, Mozambique. *Azania* 11, 25-48.

Jopela, A. (2014) – Custódia Tradicional do Património Cultural Imóvel In: Albino Jopela (Coord.) *Manual de Conservação do Património Cultural Imóvel em Moçambique, Maputo,* Ministério da Cultura, D.N.P.C. 79p.

Macamo, S. L. (1996) – The problems of conservation of archaeological sites in Mozambique. In: Pwiti, G. & Soper, R. (Eds.) *Aspects of African Archaeology: papers from the 10th Congress of the Pan African Association for Prehistory and related Studies*, 813-816. Harare: University of Zimbabwe Publications.

Macamo, S. (2006) – *Privileged Places in South Central Mozambique: The Archaeology of Manyikeni, Niamara, Songo and Degue-Mufa.* Uppsala: Department of Archaeology and Ancient History, *Studies in Global Archaeology* 4, 300p.

Macamo, S. L. (2011a) – Prosseguimento das pesquisas arqueológicas no Distrito de Massingir: Origem da criação do gado bovino np Vale do Limpopo-Rio dos Elefantes. *The Scientific Reporter* 8, 24-27.

Macamo, S. L. (2011b) – *Privileged Places in South Central Mozambique. The Archaeology of Manyikeni, Niamara, Songo and Degue-Mufa.* (second edition) VDM Publishing House (invitation by VDM Publishing House Ltd (now International Book Market Service Ltd. In cooperation with: VDM Verlag Dr. Muller GmbH. & Co.KG.

Macamo, S. L. (Coord.) (2014) – Ilha de Moçambique, Património Mundial. Maputo, Ministério da Cultura, D.N.P.C.

Macamo, S. L. & T. Saetersdal (2004) – Archaeology and cultural heritage management in Mozambique: some experiences made and some future challenges. In: *Combining the Past and the Present: archaeological perspectives on society: proceedings from the conference 'Pre-history in a global perspective' held in Bergen, August 31st – September 2nd 2001, in honour of Professor Randi Haaland's 60th anniversary*, Oestigaard T., N. Anfinset & T. Saetersdal (eds.), 189-200. Oxford: British Archaeological Report.

Macamo, S. L. & A. Ekblom (2005) – Projectos SAREC e a participação das comunidades locais na pesquisa arqueológica: O caso do distrito de Vilankulo, província de Inhambane, Moçambique. In: Benigna Zimba & José P. Castiano (Coord.) *As Ciências Sociais na Luta Contra a Pobreza.* Departamento de História, Universidade Eduardo Mondlane, Maputo. Organization for Social Science Research in Eastern and Southern Africa (OSSRE): 125-137.

Macamo, S. & J. Risberg (2007) – The Archaeology of Massingir, Gaza Province, Southern Mozambique. Gilbert Pwiti, Chantal Radimilahy & Felix Chami (Eds.), Settlements, Economies and Technology in the African past. *Studies in the African Past* 6: 67-82.

Macamo S. Risberg, J. & Ekblom A. (2011) – The Archaeology of Afro-Portuguese Settlements and Site Formation Process in the Zambezi Valley, Mozambique. *Zimbabwean Prehistory,* 29: 38-53.

Macamo, S. & B. Machava (2011) – An archaeological analysis of pottery from Massingir. *The South African Archaeological Bulletin*, 66, 194: 113-20.

Mercader, J., Y. Asmeron, T. Bennett, M. Raja & A. Skinner (2009) – Initial excavation and dating of Ngalue Cave: A Midle Stone Age Site along the Niassa Rift, Mozambique. *Journal of Human Evolution* 57: 63-74.

Mercader, J.; T. Bennett & M. Raja (2008) – Middle Stone Age starch acquisition in the Niassa Rift, Mozambique. Quaternary Research 70: 283-300. Morais, J. M. & P. J. J. Sinclair 1980. Manyikeni, a Zimbabwe in southern Mozambique. In: Leakey, R. E. & Ogot, B. A. (Eds.), *Proceedings, 8th Panafrican Congress of Prehistory and Quaternary Studies* 351-4. Nairobi: International Louis Leakey Memorial Institute for African Prehistory.

Mercader, J.; T. Bennett, C. Esselmont, S. Simpson & D. Walde (2009) – Phytoliths in woody plants from Miombo woodlands of Mozambique. *Annals of Botany:* 1-23.

Muocha, M. (2005) – *O uso das placas para a identificação do património arqueológico: estudo de caso das estações arqueológicas do Distrito de Vilankulo,* 1943-2004. Dissertação de Licenciatura. Maputo: DH/UEM.

Muocha, M. (2014) – A Educação Patrimonial no Contexto da Gestão do Património Cultural Imóvel. In: A. Jopela (Coord.) *Manual de Conservação do Património Cultural Imóvel em Moçambique,* Maputo, Ministério da Cultura, D.N.P.C.: 59-71.

Ndoro, W. (2001) – Your monuments our Shrine: the preservation of Great Zimbabwe. *Studies in African Archaeology* 19. Uppsala: Department of Archaeology and Ancient History, Uppsala University. 143p.

Sinclair, P. J. J. (1982) – Chibuene: an early trading site in southern Mozambique. *Paideuma* 28, 149-64.

Sinclair, P. (1987) – *Space, Time and Social Formation: a territorial approach to the archaeology and anthropology of Zimbabwe and Mozambique c. 0-1700 AD.* (AUN 9). Uppsala: Societas Archaeologica Upsaliensis.

Sinclair, P. (1995) – The origins of urbanism in east and southern Africa: a diachronic perspective. In: Ådahl, K. & B. Sahlström (Eds.), *Islamic Art and Culture in Sub-Saharan Africa*, 99-110. Uppsala: Acta Universitatis Uppsaliensis.

Sinclair, P. (1997) – Human Responses and Contributions to Environmental Change in Africa. In: (B. Sitter-Liver & C. Uehlinger (Eds.) *Partnership in Archaeology: perspectives of a cross-cultural dialogue. Partnership in Archaeology: perspectives of a cross-cultural dialogue*: *14th Symposium (1994) of the Swiss Academy of Humanities and Social Sciences in cooperation with the Swiss-Liechtenstein Foundation for archaeological research abroad. With the Participation of UNESCO*, 179-200. Fribourg: Fribourg University Press.

Sinclair, P. (1999) – Urban Origins in Eastern Africa. In: *The City, Local Tradition and Global Destiny*: *a seminar on urban cultural heritage (September 21-25, 1998)*, 57-62. Stockholm: Swedish International Development Cooperation Agency.

Sinclair, P.; Shaw, T. & Andah, B. (1993) – Introduction. *The Archaeology in Africa. Food, Metals and Towns.* pp. 1-31, London.

Nr.	Research Project	Scientific Results	Comments
01	Stone Age sites in Southern Mozambique	Meneses, M.P.G. 1999. *New Methodological Approaches to the Study of the Acheulean from Southern Mozambique*. New Brunswick, New Jersey: Graduate School-New Brunswick Rutgers, The State University of New Jersey	PhD dissertation
02	The Archaeological Stone Enclosures of Mozambique	Liesegang, G. 1995. *Relatório sobre a viagem a Songo, na Província de Tete, 28 de Maio a 2 de Junho de 1995*. Maputo: Departamento de Arqueologia e Antropologia, Universidade Eduardo Mondlane. Solange Macamo & Domingos Fernando. 1998. Relatório dos Trabalhos Arqueológicos no Songo. Macamo, S.L., J. Sundström & A. Ekblom 1996. Preliminary report on excavations at Songo Ruins, in Tete province Mozambique. Maputo: Department of Archaeology and Anthropology, Eduardo Mondlane University.	Report
03-4	Afro- Portuguese Settlements in the Zambezi Valley and Manica Highlands (Macamo *et al.* 2011)	Macamo S.L. & Risberg, J. 2001. Field work report in the Zambezi Valley/Mozambique (28 May to 4 June 2001). Maputo: Departamento de Arqueologia e Antropologia, Universidade Eduardo Mondlane. Baúque, G. 2002. *Trabalho de campo IV, Degue, Província de Tete, Moçambique.* Maputo: Eduardo Mondlane University, Department of Geology. Unpublished report in possession of the author.	Report
05-8	Late Stone Age and Early Iron Age settlement pattern studies in the hinterland and inland of Mozambique	Archaeological Survey and an Environmental Impact Study of a proposed by SASOL natural gas pipeline between Temane & Ressano Garcia in Mozambique (Adamowicz, 2011a); Archaeological Survey and an Environmental Impact Study in Moamba Major Project área IMPACTO/Direcção Nacional das Águas (Adamowicz, 2011a); Archaeological Survey and an Environmental Impact Study in Mabote, Inhassoro and Vilanculus Districts, IMPACTO/ SASOL (Adamowicz, 2011b); Archaeological Survey and an Environmental Impact Study Palma (Penínsulas Afungi i Cabo Delgado), IMPACTO/ ANADARKO (Adamowicz, 2011c).	See bibliography
09	Long term vegetation dynamics of Limpopo National park, focusing on paleoecological data	Ekblom A. 2011. Fieldwork report, Limpopo National Park:11.11.2011-02.12.2011	Report and publications (Ekblom & Gillson 2010a; 2010b; 2010c; Ekblom *et al.* 2011)
10	Changalane Cave	Kohtamaki, M. 2010. Different forms of interactions between Late Stone Age hunter gatherers and Early Farming Communities	Project application
11	Nacala Corridor, Vale Moçambique Lda	Luciana Paula Ribeiro de Jesus-Survey of Nacala Corridor, within the area of intervention for the railway within the Vale Corridor (Nacala- Entre Lagos) and Moatize, 2010.	Rescue archaeological project application This includes archaeological, historical and architectural heritage
12	Rock art sites and lithic artifacts.	Muianga, D. 2008-2009. Proposta de Formação. Arte Rupestre e Cultura Materail Antiga na Barragem de Cahora Bassa, Província de Tete, Moçambique	Project application
13	Quirimbas: the external Swahili influence, Islamic oriental contact and trade in the Indian Ocean inter-cultural contact.	Stepehns, C. 2006. Querimba Islands Archaeology. A Contribution to Moçambique, East African and Indian Ocean World Heritage: A Proposal to Survey the Historic Resources of Quirimba, Ibo and Matemo Islands (I)	Project application

Nr.	Research Project	Scientific Results	Comments
14-15	Midlle Stone Age in Lago and Sanga Districts, within the Rift Valley The Prehistory of Mozambique, between Lower Zambezi and Rovuma, recovery of new sites in the caves and open-air sites	Julio Mercader- Gestor do projecto. PAC-Património arqueológico e cultural da província de Niassa. Relatório das Actividades de pesquisas, 2007. Mercader, J. 2009. Relatório das pesquisas arqueológicas no Niassa. Projecto de pesquisas arqueológicas no Niassa/ A Idade da Perda Média.	Report and publications (Mercader *et al.* 2008, 2009, 2009)
16	Analysis of socio cultural practice related to heritage management of rock art sites	Jopela, A. 2009. Custódia Tradicional do Património Arqueológico em Moçambique: o caso das pinturas rupestres na Província de Manica: Projecto de pesquisa apresentado em cumprimento parcial dos requisitos exigidos para a obtenção do grau de Mestrado em Arqueologia por dissertação.	Project application
17	The Zambezi Valley project	Hilário Madiquida. The transition from Late Stone Age to Early Iron Age	Project application
18	Rock art sites in Central Mozambique	Tore Saetersdal. Projecto de Pesquisa Arqueológica e Gestão Cultural em Moçambique. Relatório Técnico Anual de 2004.	Report
19	Middle Stone Age	Nuno Ferreira Bicho. A Idade da Pedra Média e as origens do Homem Anatomicamente Moderno em Moçambique Relatório Anual de 2014	Report
20	Stone and Iron Age Sites	Hilário Madiquida. The protection of the construction area of the railway Moatize Zobwe (Vale Moçambique Lda Nacala Corridor Project)	Rescue archaeology
21	Limpopo Valley: the transition period, from Early to Late Farming Communities	Solange Macamo- National Project Coordinator of the African Archaeology Network (AAN) progress reports, 2006-2008	AAN progress reports and publications
22	Swahili Sites	Duarte, R.T. 2012. Vale Moçambique Lda Nacala Corridor Project	Rescue archaeology
23	Maritime archaeology in Inhambane	Ricardo T. Duarte. 2014. Maritime archaeology, archaeology and museum practice: research and teaching purposes	Training project

TABLE 1. PRELIMINARY INDICATION OF THE ARCHAEOLOGICAL PERMITS ISSUED BETWEEN 1994 AND 2014 (COMPILE BY S. MACAMO, 2014)

L'archéologie dans la nomenclature des sciences: approche structurelle et nouvel ordre en Côte d'Ivoire

Kouassi Kouakou Siméon
Archéologue enseignant-chercheur, Département d'Archéologie de l'Institut des Sciences, Anthropologiques de Développement (ISAD, Université Félix Houphouët-Boigny
kksimeon@yahoo.fr

Résumé
Philippe Jockey dans l'Avant-propos de son ouvrage L'Archéologie (1998) écrit: « L'archéologie est à la mode. Ce constat, établi il y a quelque vingt ans par un archéologue de renom, est aujourd'hui plus qu'hier encore d'actualité. Pourtant, le malentendu autour duquel ce phénomène de civilisation s'est construit perdure. Il existe, de fait, dans notre société moderne, une sorte de décalage entre l'image mythique que le grand public se fait de l'archéologie, l'attrait qu'elle exerce par ce biais, et la réalité quotidienne des pratiques archéologiques ». Ces propos s'adaptent parfaitement à l'environnement actuel de l'archéologie, principalement en Afrique de l'ouest francophone. Pour mieux appréhender ce paradoxe, nous décrivons l'évolution de la discipline dans le contexte de la Côte d'Ivoire. L'étude s'appuie sur le dépouillement de résultats d'enquêtes diverses, de sources d'archives et de textes de lois. Il s'agit in fine de présenter la spécificité de la gestion du patrimoine archéologique du pays et le rôle que joue l'Etat dans ce processus.

Mots-clés
Patrimoine archéologique, Politique culturelle, Etat, Nation

Abstract
Philippe Jockey in the foreword of his book Archaeology (1998) wrote: 'Archaeology is fashionable. This finding established twenty years ago by a renowned archaeologist, is today even more than yesterday a topical question. Yet the misunderstanding around which this phenomenon of civilization is built continues. There are, in fact, in our modern society, a surprising gap between the mythical image that the general public is of archeology, its appeal through this, and the daily reality of archaeological practice. 'The perception of archeology as caricatured above, eloquently translated the environment that surrounds this discipline especially in francophone West Africa. To better understand this paradox, we get down describing the evolution of the discipline in the context of Côte d'Ivoire. The study is based on the analysis results of surveys of populations and texts. This approach allows us to understand the specificity of the management of the archaeological heritage of the country and the role of the state in this process.

Key-words
Archaeological heritage, Heritage policy, State, Nation

Introduction

L'avènement de l'archéologie en Côte d'Ivoire remonte à 1903, l'instigation des amateurs de cette science. En effet, durant les années 1968-1969, à l'instigation de Claude Hélène Perrot, alors historienne à l'Université d'Abidjan, la région d'Agboville et les îles Eotilées (dans le sud) seront classées zones archéologiques. Avec la création de l'Institut d'Histoire, d'Art et d'Archéologie Africains (IHAAA) en 1974, les investigations archéologiques seront étendues à la partie Nord du pays notamment, à Kong. L'avènement de l'Institut des Sciences Anthropologiques de Développement (ISAD) en 2000 va ouvrir de nouvelles perspectives pour l'archéologie du pays, à travers notamment la création d'un Département d'archéologie destiné à former des étudiants dans cette discipline. Ce contrairement à ce qui se fait au Département d'Histoire de la même université.

Dans cette réflexion, nous tenterons de présenter le contexte de l'archéologie en Côte d'Ivoire, à travers les textes officiels, des témoignages divers et des sources d'archives. Chemin faisant, nous présenterons la politique culturelle de la Côte d'Ivoire, le cadre normatif de l'archéologie dans ce pays, et les nouvelles orientations dans cette discipline.

La politique culturelle de la Côte d'Ivoire

Importance de la politique culturelle

Il n'y a pas de doute que culture, en tant que valeur, constitue une dimension essentielle du développement durable, de par sa place centrale, dans la promotion du bien-être de l'homme. Elle est, en effet, le point d'encrage des fondements historiques et des valeurs traditionnelles qui particularisent la société ivoirienne. La politique culturelle nationale doit donc inscrire au centre de ses préoccupations, la problématique de la création et de l'innovation dans les divers modes d'expression, et œuvrer à la sauvegarde et à la valorisation des traditions. Ce qui induit que la politique culturelle est un vecteur de civisme et de protection de la liberté culturelle. L'Etat qui la suscite a le devoir de promouvoir les bonnes mœurs et de veiller à l'harmonisation de la politique culturelle ivoirienne en conformité avec les dispositions africaines et internationales en matière de promotion culturelle. Plus concrètement le « projet de loi d'orientation portant sur la politique culturelle nationale pour un développement intégré et durable » du séminaire relatif à la politique culturelle nationale pour un développement durable organisé à Grand-Bassam en décembre 2007 a prévu la mise en place d'un programme national quinquennal de développement de la culture qui pris effet en 2010 (La Côte d'Ivoire 2010, 37-44).

Dans sa structuration, la politique culturelle, ici, dispose en son chapitre sur l'Identification, que la conservation et la promotion du patrimoine culturel national, ainsi que la sauvegarde et la valorisation du patrimoine culturel national est essentielle. Les modalités et les procédures adéquates de ces opérations de sauvegarde et de valorisation sont précisées. Elles s'apprécient en termes de tenue des archives dans les ministères et structures décentralisées de l'administration, de diffusion et de promotion de la culture ivoirienne par le biais des Technologies de l'Information et de la Communication (TIC), d'aménagement culturel du territoire à travers la construction de monuments, d'habitations et d'infrastructures publics inspirés du patrimoine culturel national et de faits marquants de l'histoire de la Côte d'Ivoire. Aussi au niveau de l l'appui à la création, est-il précisé que l'Etat ivoirien, les collectivités territoriales, les opérateurs économiques, les personnes physiques ou morales, les ONG doivent apporter leur contribution au développement culturel du pays par une aide à la création pouvant se traduire par un allègement fiscal pour encourager le secteur privé et les mécènes à soutenir la vie culturelle ; la création d'un fonds destiné au soutien des opérateurs culturels, au renforcement de leurs capacités et à la structuration du secteur. Au titre de la Promotion culturelle et de l'Homme, il est préconisé la diffusion des produits artistiques, le développement du tourisme et des Industries culturelles, de la communication. Pour leur intelligibilité; la pluridisciplinarité, la création d'une université régionale ou sous régionale de recherche et d'action culturelle, la mise en place de sociétés savantes ; sont envisagées (Tailly & Alleman, 2010, 37-44)[1]. La conduite de ce chapitre important de la politique gouvernementale est du ressort du Ministère à charge de la culture.

Le Ministère de la Culture et de la Francophonie maître-d 'ouvrage de la politique culturelle

Le Ministère de la Culture et de la Francophonie dans la mise en œuvre de ses programmes s'appuie sur une organisation spécifique. Elle lui permet de collaborer avec d'autres ministères et services (Décret n°2011-277/10 du 28 septembre 2011 portant organisation du Ministère de la Culture et de Francophonie). Plus spécifiquement, et pour ce qui lui est propre, on retient (Article 1) qu'il dispose, outre le Cabinet ; de Services rattachés, d'un Secrétariat Général, de Directions Centrales et de Services Extérieurs; qu'il est chargé d'organiser par arrêté. Au Chapitre 1'portant sur la composition du cabinet (Article 3) on note au titre des Services rattachés :

[1] www.nodusciendi.net/telecharger.php?file=LaPolitiqueCulturelle.pdf

- L'Inspection Générale ;
- Le Service de la Réglementation et du Contentieux ;
- Le Service de la Communication et de la Documentation ;
- La Brigade de Lutte contre la Fraude et la Piraterie des Œuvres Culturelles ;
- Le Service de la Planification et du Suivi-Evaluation.

Les services en rapport avec le patrimoine culturel en général, sont le Service de la Réglementation et du Contentieux, la Brigade de Lutte contre la Fraude et la Piraterie des œuvres culturelles. Concernant le Service de la Réglementation et du Contentieux (Article 5) il est chargé de :

- Gérer les contentieux du Ministère et de veiller à la protection des droits d'auteurs et
- Des œuvres de l'esprit ;
- Constituer la documentation des textes juridiques ;
- Produire toute réglementation concernant les métiers, professions et services liés à
- L'activité culturelle, artistique, cinématographique ou audiovisuelle, et toutes autres activités commerciales ou industrielles liées au secteur culturel ;
- Traiter toute question d'ordre juridique et fiscal intéressant le Ministère.

Il faudrait, cependant, souligner que, jusqu'ici ce service n'est pas intervenu dans le cadre des pillages des sites archéologiques qui sont légion. Quant à la Brigade de Lutte contre la Fraude et la Piraterie des œuvres Culturelles (Article 7) elle est une unité administrative de lutte contre la fraude et la piraterie dans les activités industrielles, commerciales ou de services directement ou indirectement liées aux œuvres artistiques et culturelles. La Brigade est dirigée par un Chef de Brigade assisté de deux Sous-Directeurs. Nommés respectivement par décret pris en Conseil des Ministres et par arrêté. Ils ont rang de Directeur et de Sous-Directeur de l'administration. Outre ces services, sont érigées des directions centrales dirigées par des Directeurs nommés par décret pris en Conseil des Ministres. Ils ont rang de Directeur d'Administration Centrale à savoir :

- La Direction des Affaires Administratives et Financières ;
- La Direction des Infrastructures et des Equipements Culturels ;
- La Direction du Patrimoine Culturel ;
- La Direction de la Promotion des Arts et de la Culture ;
- La Direction de la Formation Artistique et Culturelle ;
- La Direction du Cinéma et des Industries Culturelles ;
- La Direction de la Francophonie et de la Coopération Culturelle ;
- La Direction du Livre et de la Lecture.

Les directions qui retiennent notre attention ici sont la Direction des Infrastructures et des Equipements Culturels, la Direction de la Promotion des Arts et de la Culture, la Direction de la Formation Artistique et Culturelle, la Direction du Patrimoine Culturel[2]. La Direction des Infrastructures et des Equipements Culturels est chargée de (Article 11):

- Mener les études techniques, les travaux de conservation et de restauration ;
- Assurer le contrôle et le suivi des chantiers ;
- Créer et d'équiper les centres culturels intégrés d'intérêt national ;
- Promouvoir les métiers de l'architecture liés aux arts et à la culture territoriale de la
- Culture architecturale en liaison avec les collectivités et les autres partenaires ;
- Promouvoir la qualité architecturale des bâtiments d'Etat, la décoration des espaces et
- Des bâtiments publics en œuvres d'art nationales et l'insertion des signes d'identité culturelle nationale dans les projets publics ;
- Inciter les promoteurs et constructeurs de logements à valoriser les matériaux locaux à

[2] Pour des questions d'organisation pratique, la Direction du Patrimoine Culturel sera traitée dans le chapitre portant sur l'inventaire général.

- Caractère culturel dans leurs projets.

La Direction de la Promotion des Arts et de la Culture (Article 14) a pour mission de :

- Définir la politique générale de la formation ;
- Planifier, de mettre en œuvre et d'évaluer l'organisation et le fonctionnement des structures d'enseignement artistique et culturel ;
- Coordonner les activités des structures de formation ;
- Élaborer une politique de formation dans les domaines des arts et de la culture, d'en
- Assurer l'exécution, le suivi et l'évaluation ;
- Promouvoir la formation continue et le perfectionnement des agents et du personnel d'encadrement ;
- Assurer les modalités de mise en stage en Côte d'Ivoire et à l'extérieur.

La Direction de la Formation Artistique et Culturelle (Article 16) a pour rôle de :

- Promouvoir les échanges internationaux en matière culturelle ;
- Assurer le suivi de l'évaluation des opérations de Coopération culturelle en Côte d'Ivoire ;
- Réaliser la veille culturelle en collaboration avec les attachés culturels auprès des Ambassades de Côte d'Ivoire à l'étranger ;
- Encourager et de favoriser la vie culturelle et de promouvoir une identité culturelle pour
- Une meilleure appropriation de la culture nationale dans le cadre de la diversité culturelle entre les nations.

Cette Direction de la Formation Artistique et Culturelle comprend trois Sous-Directions que sont la Sous-Direction de la Francophonie et des Relations avec les institutions, la Sous-Direction de l'intégration Culturelle et Artistique et la Sous-Direction de la Promotion de l'identité Culturelle Nationale. Les Sous-directeurs sont nommés par arrêté. L'un des objectifs de cette organisation est un maillage suffisamment important du territoire condition d'un inventaire exhaustif du patrimoine national. La Direction du Patrimoine Culturel et les structures externes exerçant sur l'ensemble du pays sont en grande partie chargés du succès de l'opération.

La question de l''inventaire général et du classement du patrimoine

La Direction du Patrimoine Culturel (Article 12) est chargée de :

- Recenser, de conserver, de préserver et de valoriser les sites et monuments historiques ;
- Promouvoir le patrimoine culturel immatériel ;
- Collecter, classifier, protéger, conserver et restaurer les objets historiques du
- Patrimoine national et les pièces ou objets provenant des recherches archéologiques ;
- Développer le patrimoine muséologique national et d'en faciliter le libre accès ;
- Mettre en œuvre la protection et la valorisation des centres urbains et quartiers anciens d'intérêt historique ou esthétique ;
- Protéger les abords des monuments historiques et de promouvoir la politique des zones de protection architecturale, urbaine et patrimoniale ;
- Assurer la restauration des immeubles protégés au titre des monuments historiques.

Ces actions peuvent se décliner en six séquences distinctes mais intimement liées comprenant l'inventaire général des sites archéologiques, la création et le développement de réserves archéologiques, les études et travaux de conservation et de restauration des matériaux recueillis, le montage d'expositions régulières, permanentes ou temporaires (musées et centres d'interprétation), la diffusion et l'animation autour du patrimoine archéologique (publications spécialisées, articles de presse, émissions radiophoniques et télévisées), l'utilisation économique et sociale du patrimoine archéologique (développement du tourisme de découverte et ses retombées sociales) (Sekongo, 2013).

Cette Direction comprend deux Sous-Directions à savoir la Sous-Direction des Musées, des sites et monuments et la Sous-Direction des Arts, des Traditions Populaires et de la Promotion des Langues Nationales.

Les services extérieurs (Article 18) qui complètent l'organisation structurelle du Ministère de la Culture et de la Francophonie comprennent les Directions Régionales, les Représentations Culturelles à l'étranger, les Musées de Côte d'Ivoire, les Centres Culturels, la Bibliothèque Nationale.

Par ces canaux, le Ministère est présent dans toutes les régions (Tailly & Alleman, 2010, 37-44) à travers ses Directions Régionales: Lagunes, Moyen, Comoé, San- Pedro, Bondoukou, Man, Abengourou, Korhogo, Bouaké, Daloa, Gagnoa où est appliquée la politique culturelle décidée par le Ministère. Dans ces régions le travail se fait en étroite collaboration avec les parties prenantes dans l'aménagement du territoire (la gestion des sites, l'animation culturelle dans les espaces urbains et ruraux), l'insertion sociale: la politique culturelle, au même titre que l'instruction publique; la décentralisation de l'administration et la vie locale.

Au titre des autres structures, le Ministère de la Culture et de la Francophonie est aidé dans sa tâche par le Ministère du Tourisme et de l'Artisanat. Il intervient dans le recensement, l'aménagement et l'exploitation des sites et monuments d'intérêt touristique et la promotion de l'artisanat et des entreprises artisanales. De même, par le biais du Ministère de la Communication, il bénéficie d'une visibilité à l'extérieur. Avec cet appareillage administratif, on comprend que le patrimoine constitue un des secteurs essentiels d'intervention du Département de la Culture.

En effet, le Patrimoine Culturel bien inventorié peut contribuer à insuffler une dynamique au secteur touristique, au transport, à l'hôtellerie, à la restauration, au commerce, aux impôts et à l'industrie. Le Patrimoine Culturel peut participer à la construction d'un citoyen accompli c'est-à-dire doté de valeurs morales et sociales indéniables enracinées dans les valeurs héritées des ancêtres fondateurs. Il suffit pour cela que soit mis en application la loi de 1987 qui établit formellement en son article 4 l'inventaire du Patrimoine Culturel National et sa révision annuelle (Koffi, 2008, 29).

Le cadre normatif de l'archéologie en Côte d'Ivoire

Le cadre normatif de l'archéologie en Côte d'Ivoire n'est pas contenu dans un document unique. L'archéologie ivoirienne oscille entre recherche scientifique et conservation patrimoniale, ce qui lui confère une situation administrative ambivalente. En 1969, est signé le décret n°69-303 du 4 juillet 1969 portant création de l'Institut d'Histoire d'Art et d'Archéologie Africains (IHAAA) auprès de l'Université d'Abidjan, alors sous tutelle de l'Education nationale. Il y est attribué à l'institut (Article 2 du décret) une vocation d'enseignement et de recherches, la formation des chercheurs, la prospection du pays, la conservation et la diffusion des découvertes sur l'histoire ancienne et moderne du territoire national. Avec l'ouverture en décembre 1971 d'un Secrétariat d'Etat chargé des Affaires Culturelles, qui se mue de 1976-1977 en Ministère autonome, la gestion du patrimoine archéologique lui est désormais dévolue à travers le 'Service de la protection des sites et du patrimoine historique et de l'archéologie' au détriment de l'IHAAA. Cette attribution est confirmée par la loi n°87-806 du 28 juillet 1987 (Gautier, 2002) portant protection du patrimoine culturel. Votée à l'initiative du Ministère des Affaires Culturelles, son chapitre III (Articles 37 à 45) est consacré précisément au régime des fouilles archéologiques et aux questions connexes. Des subventions étaient alors régulièrement accordées à l'IHAAA jusqu'en 1986. Aussi, la Côte d'Ivoire a-t-elle adhéré, au niveau international, à un certain nombre de recommandations et conventions parrainés par l'UNESCO. Ce sont la 'Recommandation définissant les principes internationaux à appliquer en matière de fouilles archéologiques' (1956), la 'Recommandation concernant la préservation des biens culturels mis en péril par les travaux publics ou privés' (19 novembre 1968), la 'Convention sur la protection du patrimoine culturel subaquatique' (2001) (Sekongo, 2013, 2), la 'Convention de l'UNESCO de 1970 concernant les mesures à prendre pour interdire et empêcher l'importation, l'exportation et le transfert de propriété illicites des biens culturels' (30 octobre 1990, entrée en vigueur le 30 janvier

1991) la 'Convention d'Unidroit sur les biens culturels volés ou illicitement exportés' (24 juin 1995 à Rome)[3]. Ces textes normatifs donnent un large éventail à la pratique de l'archéologie dans le pays en l'ouvrant à des missions internationales (France, Belgique, Suisse, …) et en lui garantissant ses fonctions de recherche scientifique et de conservation en matière archéologique.

Des dispositions de différents services et codes, notamment celui régissant l'environnement que nous avons déjà analysé dans un autre forum (Rencontre de la Commission « Politiques et structures de gestion du patrimoine archéologique » à Dakar du 29 au 31 mai 2013) permettent également d'appréhender les dispositifs légaux qui soutendent sa pratique sur le terrain. Il revient donc aux archéologues d'être attentifs à l'évolution de ces structures et du pays. Nous pouvons ici relever le rôle qu'est appelé à jouer le service des Douanes ivoiriennes rattaché au Ministère de l'Economie et des Finances. Pour rappel, on retient que la Direction Générale des Douanes (DGD) est chargée de faire respecter les dispositions législatives et réglementaires auxquelles sont soumis les mouvements des personnes, des marchandises, des moyens de transport et des capitaux à l'entrée et à la sortie du territoire. A ce titre, la douane exerce de nombreuses missions dont la protection du patrimoine culturel et de l'environnement par le contrôle des exportations de biens culturels[4]. A côté de ces dispositifs, qui peuvent être qualifiés de matériels parce que marqués par écrits, apparaissent d'autres plutôt immatériels régis par des lois et méthodes traditionnelles de conservation.

De façon générale, les lois traditionnelles de conservation du patrimoine culturel sont des interdits ou des secrets que détiennent une caste ou un groupe de personnes qui ne doivent pas être violés par un tiers, de même que des bois ou rivières sacrés pour les sites. Nous avons à titre d'exemple la forêt sacrée Cloetcha d'Abobo à Abidjan, qui est ce qui reste des forêts sacrées du peuple Ebrié, la forêt sacrée Topé de Grand-Bassam, l'unique forêt sacrée du royaume Abouré. Les bois sacrés, lieux d'initiation des castes, des générations se retrouvent à la fois au Sud et au Nord du pays. Les rivières sacrées, lieux d'adoration d'une communauté foisonnant au Centre, à l'Est et Nord-est de la Côte d'Ivoire (Koffi, 2008, 22). Les archéologues et les structures qui les emploient, dans le souci de rendre la discipline plus visible et la sortir du long sommeil qui l'a caractérisé de 1990 à 2000, ont opté pour une organisation plus sereine qui leur permet de plus en plus de remplir au mieux leur fonction.

Les nouvelles orientations de l'archéologie en Côte d'Ivoire

Le bilan et l'état des difficultés de la recherche archéologique en Côte d'Ivoire, à ce jour, sont contrastés. Parmi les acquis, figurent un réel progrès dans la formation des professionnels du patrimoine archéologique, chercheurs et conservateurs, de même que la reconnaissance de l'archéologie comme partie intégrante du patrimoine devant être prise en compte dans l'action publique nationale. Cependant, les mesures générales de protection et de gestion restent plus qu'insuffisantes au regard des standards internationaux : le cadre juridique souffre d'incomplétude, tout comme le cadre institutionnel ou organique ; la protection juridique et pratique des sites archéologiques est quasi inexistante (du fait de manque de décrets d'application) ; l'archéologie préventive ('archéologie de sauvetage 'loi 1987) fait défaut, de même que la mise en valeur des produits archéologiques et la concertation régulière entre les parties prenantes concernées ... Cette non appropriation globale de la gestion du patrimoine archéologique a pour conséquences notamment le développement des fouilles clandestines et la destruction de sites importants (Fanfala, région d'Odienné ; Gohitafla, Centre-ouest ; La Bété, Anyama; Songon, Nord-ouest d'Abidjan) de même que l'insécurité ambiante dans laquelle baignent les matériaux archéologiques recueillis (Sekongo, 2013, 2) qui ne sont pas toujours mis à la disposition des musées.

Tirant les leçons des difficultés rencontrées depuis sa formalisation dans les années 1968-1969, à savoir des ressources insuffisantes à son épanouissement, à un cadre juridique quasiment inexistant,

---

3 http://icom.museum/ressources/base-de-donnees-des-listes-rouges/liste-rouge/afrique/legislation/L/2/

4 http://www.douanes.ci/?page=Infos

les archéologues ont pris leurs responsabilités. Avec la création du Département d'Archéologie de l'Institut des Sciences Anthropologiques de Développement (ISAD), l'un des quatre Départements de l'Institut en 2001, une nouvelle stratégie de recherche basée sur trois laboratoires est mise en place.

Ainsi le laboratoire d'Archéologie et identité culturelle est structuré autour d'un vaste programme de prospection archéologique dont l'objectif est de définir les potentialités archéologiques de la Côte d'Ivoire. Pour cela, le programme est subdivisé en neuf (9) régions archéologiques qui constituent autant de projets. Ce sont : le nord-est, le nord-ouest, l'ouest montagneux, le sud-ouest, le centre-Ouest, le V Baoulé, l'est, le pays Sénoufo, la région des lagunes.

Le laboratoire d'Histoire des techniques, quant à lui, vise à recenser, inventorier, classer, interpréter et valoriser l'ensemble de techniques anciennes de Côte d'Ivoire : Métallurgie, Céramique, Matériaux organiques…les recherches doivent aboutir à :

- L'élaboration d'une carte des techniques anciennes ;
- L'obtention d'une chronologique cohérente ;
- Une meilleure connaissance des savoir-faire techniques des sociétés ivoiriennes précoloniales.

En outre, le laboratoire entreprend vingt-sept (27) projets dont la réalisation devrait déboucher sur un ouvrage de synthèse sur chacune des grandes techniques anciennes de Côte d'Ivoire.

Le laboratoire d'Archéologie des mondes africains contemporains enfin, est structuré autour de toutes les problématiques en relation avec la valorisation du patrimoine culturel en Côte d'Ivoire et la protection des sites en danger. Plusieurs projets ont été déjà identifiés:

- Route d'esclave ;
- Sauvegarde des sites en danger ;
- Archéologie et muséographie.

Ce programme doit permettre une meilleure diffusion du patrimoine culturel ivoirien auprès des populations. Grâce à un potentiel important d'étudiants et les travaux des enseignants-chercheurs, de nombreuses études qui couvrent assez remarquablement le pays, à partir de problématiques de recherches cohérentes sont en cours. On est en droit d'espérer que dans un futur proche des résultats intéressants qui fassent connaître la Côte d'Ivoire archéologique soient obtenus. D'ores et déjà deux thèses de doctorat issues de cette nouvelle vision de l'archéologie ont été soutenues en 2007 et 2011 sur la Côte d'Ivoire côtière et les pierres sculptées de Gohitafla. Cinq autres sont en cours et 12 mémoires de Master sont en élaboration. C'est un potentiel important de ressources humaines qui est en constitution et qui devrait permettre à terme de développer davantage l'archéologie dans le territoire. En outre des actions vigoureuses sont menées dans le sens de la sensibilisation des autorités politiques et administratives en vue de l'instauration de l'archéologie préventive. Celle-ci apparait comme une chance supplémentaire pour la redynamisation de la recherche archéologique en Côte d'Ivoire.

Conclusion

L'analyse du cadre structurel de l'archéologie en Côte d'Ivoire a mis en évidence la réorientation constatée ces dernières années. Il en découle qu'une politique culturelle efficiente devrait engager l'entité concernée à jouer pleinement son rôle. En la matière, et vu l'importance de la culture dans le développement d'un pays, il apparait inconcevable d'attendre à ce niveau des capitaux étrangers pour la financer. Il revient aux Etats de prendre leur responsabilité en vue de participer plus efficacement à la mondialisation. L'archéologie peut y contribuer en tant que levier du développement durable par rapport à sa capacité de participer de façon active au brassage des peuples et au renforcement de la cohésion sociale; car si le sens étymologique en fait, l'étude des choses anciennes, son essence réside dans une meilleure connaissance du présent.

References

Gaultier, C. (2002) – « Loi n°87-806 du 28 juillet 1987 portant protection du patrimoine culturel de Côte d'Ivoire », In: Droit et patrimoine en Afrique: Patrimoine Francophone. Université Senghor (CD-ROM), n°6, Réactualisation.

Koffi, B. Y. (2008) – Côte d'Ivoire, Communication au Salon des études en sciences sociales de l'Université Hampâté, 31p.

Tailly, A. & Alleman, I. M. (2010) – La Côte d'Ivoire. Profil culturel des pays du sud membres de la Francophonie. Un aperçu de trois pays de l'UEMOA. Le Burkina Faso, la Côte d'Ivoire, le Sénégal, Organisation Internationale de la Francophonie, pp. 33-44.

Jockey, P. (1999) – L'archéologie, Paris, Belin, 399p.

Sekongo (Y. F.), (2013) – Recherche scientifique et conservation du patrimoine. Le cas du patrimoine archéologique en Côte d'Ivoire, communication au XIIIe colloque de l'Association Ouest Africaine d'Archéologie, Abidjan.

The role of civil society in preservation of archaeological heritage in the Republic of Moldova

Sergiu Musteaţă
History and Geography Faculty, 'Ion Creanga' State University 1, Ion Creanga str., main building, of. 407, Chisinau, 2069, Republic of Moldova
sergiu_musteata@yahoo.com

Abstract

In this paper the author is discussing the role of civil society in preservation of the archaeological heritage in Republic of Moldova. Republic of Moldova signed the European Convention on Archaeological Heritage Preservation (revised version) in 1998, ratified it in 2001 and only starting with November 2002 it entered into force. But, the national law on archaeological preservation was voted by Parliament in September 2010 and entered in force in March 2011. So, after a long period of debates and initiatives Republic of Moldova has its own law on this field. The leading role in this process had the National Association of Young Historians of Moldova. This NGO initiated in 2009 an advocacy project in the field of cultural heritage preservation. As main goal and result was the elaboration a new law on archaeological heritage preservation, based on European an International Convention and actual trends in the field of archaeological heritage preservation.

Key words

Archaeological Heritage Preservation, Civil Society, Republic of Moldova

Résumé

Dans cet article, l'auteur discute du rôle de la société civile dans la préservation du patrimoine archéologique en République de Moldovie. La République de Moldovie a signé la Convention européenne sur la préservation du patrimoine archéologique (version révisée) en 1998, l'a ratifiée en 2001 et elle ne l'a mise en application qu'en novembre 2002. Mais la loi nationale sur la préservation archéologique a été votée par le Parlement en septembre 2010 et est entrée en vigueur en mars 2011. Ainsi, après une longue période de débats et d'initiatives, la République de Moldovie eut sa propre loi dans ce domaine. L'Association nationale des jeunes historiens de Moldova a joué un rôle de premier plan dans ce processus. Cette ONG a lancé en 2009 un projet de plaidoyer dans le champ de la préservation du patrimoine culturel. Elle eut pour principal but et résultat l'élaboration d'une nouvelle loi sur la préservation du patrimoine archéologique, basée sur la Convention Européenne et Internationale et sur les tendances actuelles dans le domaine de la préservation du patrimoine archéologique.

Mots-clés

Préservation du Patrimoine Archéologique, Société Civile, République de Moldavie

Introduction

The National Association of Young Historians of Moldova – ANTIM, founded in 1997, is a non-political, non-profit association, which has the public benefit as a purpose. By establishing the ANTIM, its founders primarily wanted to meet a social need, by promoting national and international collaboration of young people that stimulates research activities and helps to preserve our cultural national inheritance. ANTIM is an organization that succeeded to affirm itself through multiple projects that cover various area of historical research. It is widely recognized for its scientifically and practical activities, for the initiation and organization of many symposiums, conferences, summer schools and some more ample academic activities.[1] Among ANTIM successful activities was the 2009-2010 project '*The policy of archaeological heritage preservation in the Republic of Moldova: reality*

[1] More details on ANTIM see on its web page: http://antim.md/

and necessity', supported by Soros Foundation-Moldova and Swedish Agency for Development and International Cooperation – SIDA. The project included one-year advocacy campaign – regional and national meeting, conferences, mass media information activities, publication of leaflets, posters, collection of laws, writing a project of new law on archaeological heritage preservation and its public discussion, including with international experts, etc.

From a project idea to a project law

Republic of Moldova got its Independency in August 1991. Its first Law on cultural heritage preservation was approved in 1993 – the law on monuments' preservation. This law is very general and it was poorly developed in relation to archaeological heritage. The most difficult problem was not just the content of the law, but inefficiency of the state bodies to implement it. For example, the National Register approved in 1993 was published only in 2010.

During last two decades Republic of Moldova has signed many international treaties, and from those 10 International and European Conventions on cultural heritage Republic of Moldova signed in 1998 the Granada and Valletta Conventions. But, signing these Conventions did not change the situation of Moldova in the field of cultural heritage preservation. So, after a decade of our Independency a group of scholars from Academy of Sciences of Moldova initiated a new project on cultural heritage preservation, which was not supported by the Government.

In 2005 a group of archaeologists prepared a first law draft project on archaeological heritage preservation, which was discussed for five years in various circles – civil, academic, and even political.[2] In 2009, the National Association of Young Historians of Moldova, as part of Advocacy project, took the initiative to update and promote the draft law project by involving its initial authors and other domestic[3] and foreign archaeologists, managing to propose to the Ministry of Culture an updated version in line with contemporary requirements. This project received important feedback and support from colleagues in the United States, Germany, Romania and elsewhere.[4]

Project's main purpose was to promote efficient policies for heritage conservation, having the following objectives:

- Setting a sustainable partnership with local public administration for the elaboration and implementation of some policies to protect the archaeological heritage.
- Development of a coherent long-term national strategy, which would count generally the preservation of cultural and historical heritage and the archaeological heritage, especially among national priorities.
- Improvement of national legal framework, by adoption of some laws regarding the protection of archaeological heritage.
- Discussions with the decision makers about the opportunity of establishing a viable and accountable structure in the field.

The project was launched on 15th of May 2009 at the Round Table 'Museum policies in Republic of Moldova', with the participation of a wide audience, including specialists from museum network of the country. Immediately after the launch of the project, the working group drafted the activities agenda and tasks were distributed among members. Simultaneously, letters were sent to representatives of local public administration of northern districts that were invited at the first seminar of the project. From the beginning were elaborated the leaflet and project's poster, which

[2] Authors of the 2005 project law were S. Musteață, Gh. Postică, and E. Sava.

[3] Important contributions came from O. Munteanu, I. Tentiuc, V. Vornic, V. Kavruk.

[4] I would like to thank many colleagues from abroad for useful suggestions which helped us improve the law project, including: Paul Shackel, Barbara Little, Uzi Baram (United States of America), Friederich Lüth, Alexandru Popa (Germany), Vasile Chirica, Vitalie Josanu, Viorica Crişan, A. A. Rusu, Eugen Teodor (Romania).

presented the main information about the project and facilitated the informing of the public about the purposes, objectives and further activities.

During the period May 2009 – May 2010, according to the action plan, were performed a range of activities, structured in three main directions:

The analysis and evaluation of protection policies of archaeological heritage

The project has been accomplished in two successive stages: at regional and national level. In first stage, we organised three regional meetings (north, centre and south), attended by approximately 100 representatives of local public administration and district museums. At these meetings was discussed the real situation of each district and were searched solutions to improve the situation. Also at these meetings were presented the objectives and the activities of the project and were discussed the projects of national strategy and the law for archaeological heritage preservation in Republic of Moldova. The first meeting took place in Bălți on 16th of June 2009, the second in Chisinau on 1st of October and the third in Cahul, on 8th of October 2010.

Lobby and promotion of cultural policies changes

In the second stage were organised working meetings with the representatives of Government and Parliament where was discussed the situation of the archaeological heritage in Republic of Moldova. The project director and a few members of the working group (Gh. Postică, E. Sava, I. Ştefăniţă) had some meetings in October with Mr. Focşa, the then minister of culture and discussed about the problems of cultural heritage situation, especially the archaeological heritage. The Draft Law was presented by the Ministry of Culture and further supported by the Government through a decision submitted in Parliament. On the Round Table, on 9th March 2010, were discussed the Law Draft of archaeological heritage preservation with members of parliamentary Committee for Culture, Education and Mass Media. The project working team found a real support from the Parliamentary Committee, being ensured of supporting this project to be included in Parliament agenda. Further, after receiving the opinions about the law draft from the Parliamentary Committee, the working group met again with the representatives of Juridical Committee and Committee for Culture, Education and Mass Media, where were embodied some details. Final conclusion was that most of the opinions of the parliamentary committees were positive and the suggestions are beneficial for the law draft.

The final conference, that took place on 20th of May 2010 and had 40 representatives from different governmental institutions, including from Ministry of Culture, General Prosecutor, Ministry of Internal Affairs, Hall of Chisinau, universities and others. Representatives from Ministry of Internal Affairs and General Prosecutor showed interest towards the problems that were discussed and stated the availability for further collaboration and exchange of information in the field of cultural heritage preservation of Republic of Moldova.

Mass media campaigns

The project was supported by an information campaign to raise the public awareness on the necessity to adopt an efficient protection policy for archaeological heritage. So, we made a series of radio shows, we published a lot of articles in the national written mass media about the problems discussed in the project (copies of the articles are attached). Also, we developed and distributed leaflets, posters and two compilations of normative acts and international conventions that facilitated the disclosure of the population about the problems approached in the project.

On 13th of April 2010, was organized a round table with the participation of Mr. Vitalie Josanul, officer in heritage police of Neamţ county, who presented the experience of Romania in fighting against the violations that leads to damages or destructions of historical heritage. The approached subject attracted the Mass Media interest and was highly mediated.

Final results

The following project's objectives were met:

1. As a result of the change of government in the summer-autumn of 2009 we succeeded to establish a qualitative partnership as some experts from the project were appointed to responsible governmental positions that facilitated the achievement of the proposed objectives. This change fortified the relationship with the representatives of local public administration which in the period of communist governance were less receptive to our goals.
2. In agreement with the representatives from Culture Ministry and Parliamentary Committee for Culture, we completed the law draft regarding the preservation of archaeological heritage, which later was voted by the Parliament.
3. We elaborated the national strategy project regarding the protection of archaeological heritage and other normative acts, published in a separate compilation, which will serve as a working tool for the staff that activates in this area.
4. Within the project has been proposed the establishment of a National Archaeological Agency. The agency was created by the Government of Republic of Moldova in 2012, function and responsibilities of this agency are specified in the law on archaeological heritage preservation.
5. Within the project were elaborated two compilations of normative acts and international conventions, which are a working tool for all people interested in the protection of archaeological heritage.

Within the Campaign of advocacy, succeeded to raise the awareness of public opinion on some cases regarding the preservation of archaeological heritage. So, during the project, it was distributed two compilations of normative acts regarding the safety of archaeological heritage (Musteaţă, 2010, 2011).

Qualitative results:

1. Regional seminars fortified the collaboration with the representatives of local public administration and with museum specialists from different rural locations of the country.
2. Discussions with the representatives of the new central administration Culture Ministry, Parliamentary Committee for Culture, Education and Mass Media, Legal Committee led to drawing up a qualitative law draft, which was supported by Parliament.
3. Raising awareness of the public opinion resulted with a high mediatisation of many cases regarding the situation of the cultural heritage and especially of the archaeological one in Republic of Moldova.
4. Referral to investigation authorities (General Prosecutor), regarding the destructions of archaeological traces around the Măzărache Church from Chişinău.

Impact

1. Performed activities within the project had a directly impact on our society. As a result, we established a long-term partnership with many representatives of local public and central administration, in sight of promoting a national policy on preservation of archaeological heritage. The media campaign that raised the awareness of the public opinion, directly contributed to the discussion of some problems and cases regarding destructions and damages of cultural heritage and necessity of an efficient cultural policy. Establishment of the projects of some normative acts (strategies, laws, regulations etc.) proved the interest of the civil society, academic environment and of some politicians in implementation of an actual regulatory framework, adapted to international conventions, part of which is also Republic of Moldova.
2. Another impact of our activities was the notification of the Ministry of Culture regarding the urgent need to speed the publication in the Official Monitor of Republic of Moldova of the Register of the monuments protected by government, which even if was adopted by Parliament

in 1993, same as Law regarding preservation of the monuments, it remained unpublished and did not allow to apply the legal requirements in cases where the monuments were damaged or destroyed. In February 2010, after 17 years, the Register of monuments protected by government was published in Official Monitor which provided the normative acts needed for protecting the cultural sites.

3. The Agency of Inspection and Restoration of Monuments initiated the assessment of the state protected monuments included in the National Register, which will determine their current condition. First results of these inspections, especially in Chisinau, were widely publicized. Thus, as a result of our project, the society has been informed about the difficult condition of our archaeological heritage protection and the need of taking actions by state institutions.
4. Thanks to the wide coverage of these issues, Cultural Heritage Institute of the Academy of Science of Moldova, initiated the development of a national program on Preservation of Cultural Heritage in Republic of Moldova. Project's team has actively participated in the development of this program and highlighted the important role to be given to civil society and public involvement in solving problems of preservation and promotion of cultural heritage of Republic of Moldova.

Promotion

One of the project's priorities was Mass Media campaign. Therefore, during the project, was carried out an information campaign and public awareness on the need for an effective protection of the archaeological heritage. Thus, we managed to achieve a series of interviews on various radio and TV stations, we published several articles in national and district print media, in which were addressed issues concerning the protection of cultural heritage. We also developed, copied and distributed over 1,000 leaflets, 1,500 posters and 1,500 compilations of normative acts and international conventions and a legal guidance in an edition of 1,000 copies. All these media activities together, made the project visible and transparent, our actions being sensitized and popularized by various radio, TV and print media.

Lessons learned:

Although ANTIM has an extensive experience in implementation of projects, in the project 'Protection policies of the archaeological heritage in Republic of Moldova: reality & necessity', we have learned useful lessons for our work on, such as:

1. The partnership with state structures may be developed and must be developed continuously, providing quality services, that APL and central administration can't or fails to offer.
2. Access to information remains a problem for Moldovan citizens, including the access to information in the area of archaeological heritage protection. That's why the responsible authorities must multiply activities in this direction to improve the situation.
3. Availability of state institutions to collaborate with civil society on an equal level.

Conclusion

The Law on Archaeological Heritage Preservation was adopted by a unanimous vote, including the vote of the communist faction which traditionally being in opposition does not support any democrat initiative, by the Parliament of Republic of Moldova on 17th September 2010 and enacted by Presidential Decree on 24th November 2010.[5] The Law entered into force three months after its publication in the Official Gazette (Monitorul Oficial) of 3rd December 2010.[6] Therefore, from 3rd

[5] Decree on the enactment of the Law on Archaeological Heritage Preservation, Interim President of the Republic of Moldova Mihai Ghimpu, No. 642-V, 24 November 2010. In: Monitorul Oficial al Republicii Moldova, No. 235-240, Year XVII (376-3773), 3 December 2010, Art. 737, p. 8.

[6] Law on Archaeological Heritage Preservation (no. 218 from 17 September 2010). In: Monitorul Oficial al Republicii Moldova, No. 235-240, Year XVII (376-3773), 3 December 2010, Art. 738, pp. 8-17.

March 2011, the Republic of Moldova has had a new preservation system for its archaeological heritage. This Law is the first of its kind in the legislation of Moldova and was elaborated according to own experience, experts′ recommendations, Valletta Convention (1992) and ICOMOS Charter (1990). The Law on Archaeological Heritage Preservation of the Republic of Moldova contains 48 articles grouped into 11 chapters (Musteaţă, 2012). The Law on archaeological heritage preservation opens new perspectives for Moldovan society to improve the situation in the field, and to fight black archaeology and illegal trafficking of antiquities. With this Law the Republic of Moldova aligns itself to other European countries and honours, first of all, its commitments taken with signing the Valletta Convention, and second, other European and International Field Conventions. The preparation, discussion and the lobby process for the project law on preservation of archaeological heritage undertaken by an NGO initiative and supported by the democratic Government a serve as a good practice example of partnership between civil society and state bodies. However, a durable cooperation between these two parts is required in order to improve the situation in the field of archaeological heritage preservation.

Acknowledges

This research is part of the Project 'Current trends in archaeological heritage preservation: the national and the international perspectives', supported by CNCS –UEFISCDI, PN-II-ID-PCE-2011-3-0610. Institute of Archaeology of the Romanian Academy, Iasi branch, Romania.

Legislation

Decree on the enactment of the Law on Archaeological Heritage Preservation, Interim President of the Republic of Moldova Mihai Ghimpu, No. 642-V, 24 November 2010. In: Monitorul Oficial al Republicii Moldova (Official Gazette), No. 235-240, Year XVII (376-3773), 3 December 2010, Art. 737, p. 8.

Law on Archaeological Heritage Preservation (no. 218 from 17 September 2010). In: Monitorul Oficial al Republicii Moldova (Official Gazette), No. 235-240, Year XVII (376-3773), 3 December 2010, Art. 738, p. 8-17.

References

Musteaţă, S. (Eds.), (2001) – Protecţia Patrimoniului, Culegere de Legi şi Convenţii. Heritage Preservation. Colleaction of Laws and Conventions, Chişinău.160p.

Musteaţă, S. (2007) – Preservation of the archaeological heritage in the Republic of Moldova. Archäologisches Nachrichtenblatt, 12(4): 311-322.

Musteaţă, S. (2008) – Protecţia patrimoniului arheologic. Studiu comparativ: legislaţia Republicii Moldova şi Statelor Unite ale Americii, [Preservation of the archaeological heritage. Comparative study: the legal framework in the Republic of Moldova and the United States of America]. Monografii ANTIM IV, Chişinău: Pontos. 216p.

Musteaţă, S. (2009a) – Unele consideraţii privind Convenţia europeană pentru protecţia patrimoniului arheologic şi implementarea ei în Republica Moldova [Some considerations of the European Convention for archaeological heritage preservation and its implementation in the Republic of Moldova]. In: A. Gilaş, V. Stepanov (Redactori), Conferinţa Internaţională Ştiinţifică 'Păstrarea patrimoniului cultural în ţările europene', Chişinău, pp. 20-32.

Musteaţă, S. (2009b) – Etica şi deontologia profesională în arheologie. Tyragetia: Istorie. Muzeologie: Serie Nouă: Vol. 3 [18] 1: 353-360.

Musteaţă, S. (2009c) – Let's do our job better and then there will be no reasons to talk about relevancy of archaeology. Historical Archaeology 43 (4), 122-124.

Musteaţă, S. (Eds.) (2010a) – Protecţia juridică a patrimoniului arheologic. Culegere de acte normative şi convenţii internaţionale. Chişinău, Editura Ruxanda. 370p.

Musteaţă, S. (2010b) – Cultural Heritage Preservation in the Republic of Moldova between Legal Framework and Reality. Civilization Research, 8: 161-178, Tbilisi.

Musteaţă, S. (2011) – Looting Antiquities in the Republic of Moldova. In: E. Sava, B. Govedarica, B. Hänsel (Hrsg.), Der Schwarzmeerraum vom Äneolitikum bis in die Frühheisenzeit (5000-500 v.Chr.), Band 2, Globale Entwicklung versus Lolageschichehen. Internationale Fachtagung von Humboldtianer im Humboldt-Kolleg in Chişinău, Moldavien (4. – 8. Oktober 2010), Rehden/ Westf., Verlag Marie Leidorf GmbH, 279-284.

Musteaţă, S. (2012) – A New Law – A New Perspective for Archaeological Heritage Preservation in the Republic of Moldova. International Journal of Cultural Property, 19 (4), 2012, 535-541.

MANAGEMENT AND USE OF SCIENCE DATA FROM PREVENTIVE ARCHAEOLOGY: QUALITY CONTROL

SESSION 15 B

Edited by

Pascal Depaepe and Asya Engovatova

Quality management organisation in Inrap (France)

Alain Koehler
(Inrap)
alain.koehler@inrap.fr

Abstract
In France, archaeological surveys and excavations are the subject of technical and scientific controls of Ministry of Culture services, they are also prescribers of archaeological operations. On its side, the archaeological operator defines and controls the means, methods and techniques relevant to the achievement of objectives: in this case, Inrap is responsible for the quality of archaeological information. This quality must be assessed at all stages of the operation, from feasibility studies to the scientific exploitation of results. Inrap is committed to a quality approach, illustrated here by few examples.

Résumé
En France, la réalisation des interventions archéologiques fait l'objet d'un contrôle scientifique et technique par des services de l'Etat qui sont aussi les services prescripteurs des opérations. Mais c'est à l'opérateur de définir et contrôler les moyens, les méthodes et les techniques utiles à l'atteinte des objectifs: il est responsable de la qualité des informations archéologiques. Cette qualité doit pouvoir être évaluée à toutes les étapes de l'opération, depuis les études de faisabilité jusqu'à l'exploitation scientifique des résultats. L'Inrap est engagé dans une démarche qualité, illustrée ici par quelques exemples.

Introduction

In France, archaeological survey and excavations are subject to scientific and technical control by dedicated services of the French Ministry of Culture. Those archaeological services are prescribers for surveys and excavations. Archaeological reports are assessed by scientific commission. Thc quality of archaeological data collected should be assessed at all stages, from field to synthesis stage. Quality control has become essential in archaeology if we want to consolidate the scientific level of our discipline.

'Quality Control'

'Quality control', means 'to assess whether the service is compliant or not with the specifications or requirements for a predetermined reference. It includes an acceptance or an adjustment decision.' The 'service' concept seems well suited to what we produce and how we produce it. It is wraparound services, such as achieving an archaeological evaluation, but also services dedicated to more specific actions, such as conducting an archaeological section. The process is to compare the service performed to what was expected. It must necessarily have been formalized from a shared and endorsed repository. In the case of the evaluation of scientific intervention project, the framework is constituted by the scientific and technical specifications attached to the prefectural decision. This formalization must exist previously to the service, it does not mean it can't be adapted and revised throughout an archaeological operation. All quality control must include the fact that we discover more about the object of our study as we destroy it. This review should lead to a decision, which is to accept or not to accept the service as such, partially or with changes.

If 'touch-up' is necessary but is not possible (you can't start over the excavation of an archaeological layer), it makes sense not to accept the service. Then, it would mean an irretrievable loss of archaeological data. Therefore, archaeologists can accept a service that is non-compliant. Quality

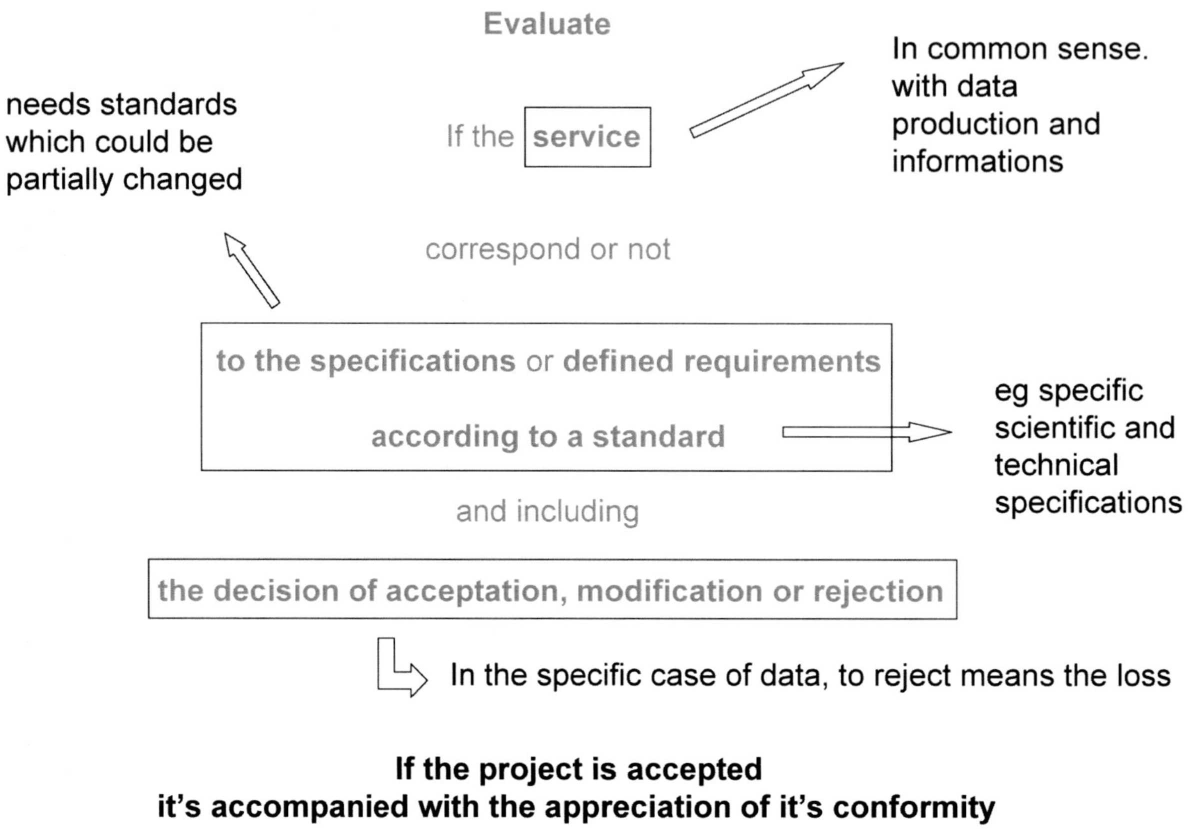

Figure 1. Quality control definition

control could be seen as flexible but it has to stand firm on the need to express the quality of data produced. We must be realistic: this process is not implemented actually. Reports, papers and monographs are in their vast majority published without being accompanied by this quality control.

To ensure 'quality' (of Inrap)

This public institute was first an association created in 1973. It was called AFAN and at that time, its primary role was to manage the resources needed for the realization of archaeological surveys directly decided between the state and the land developers.

Surveys and excavations made on major land projects raised questions of organization and standardization, especially on the technical aspects (surveying, finalized documents and reports). In some cases, benchmarks, models, even charters were created, allowing the first steps of quality control. These approaches remain specific to each operation. But after the 2001 Act (which has settled Inrap in the heart of preventive archaeology device) this need for improvement became vital and indispensable for all preventive interventions.

National archaeological legislation changes in 2003, introducing competition in the field of diagnosis (only public operators) and excavations (public and private operators). This new deal has forced an active engagement to accelerate the progress made towards a better controlled quality for Inrap operations.

Inrap annually conducts around 1500 archaeological evaluations and over 250 excavations in France and overseas departments. Its threefold legislative mission is:

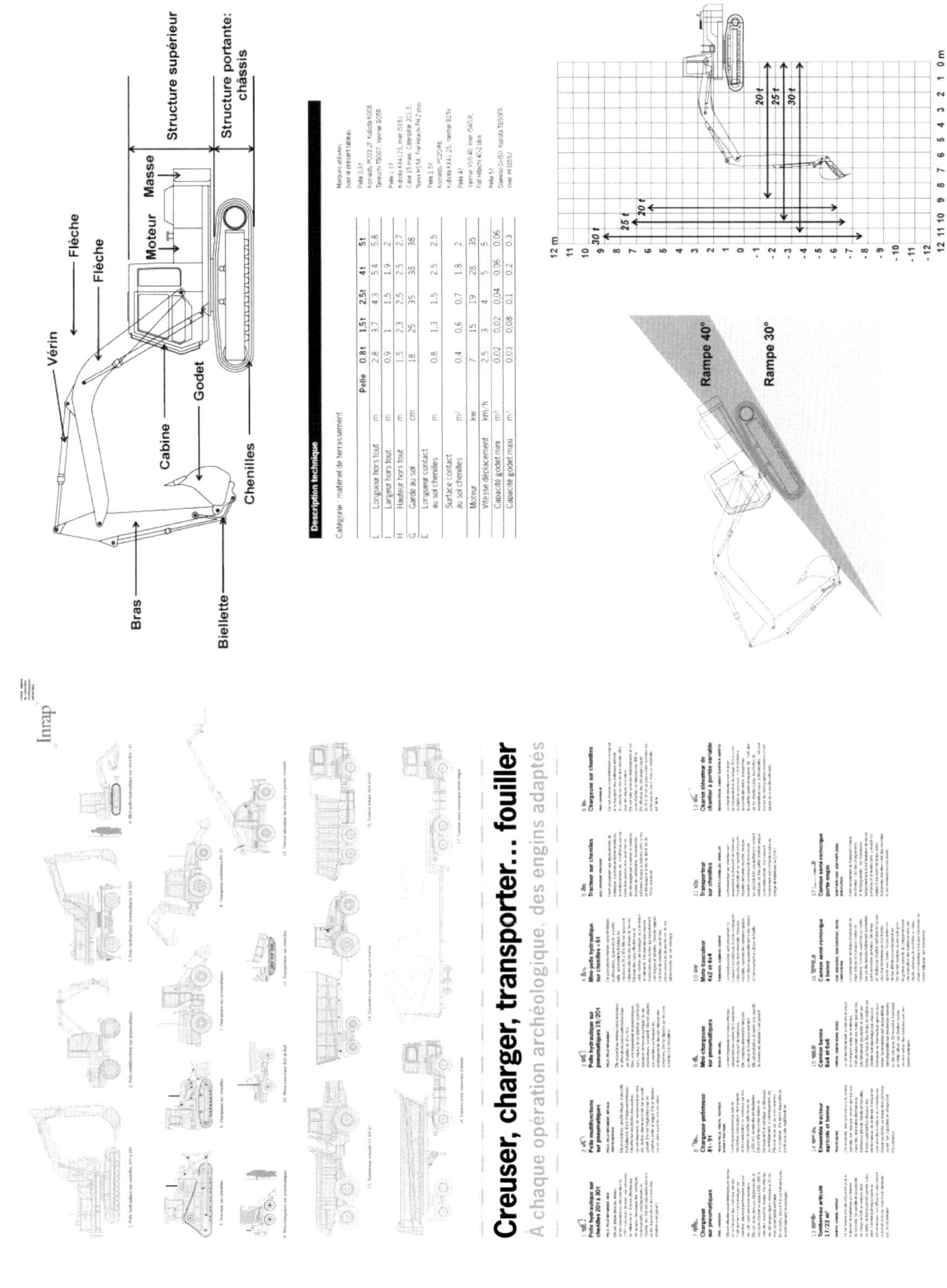

FIGURE 2. 'TO DIG, TO CHARGE, TO TRANSPORT… TO EXCAVATE'. OFFICIAL TERMINOLOGY, USE AND KNOWLEDGE OF THE FUNCTION OF MECHANICAL DIGGERS AND OTHER DEVICE. ALL CONSTITUTE ELEMENTARY BASIS OF ARCHAEOLOGICAL FIELD WORK

– Inrap is an operator for diagnostic and preventive archaeology excavations (projects and studies);
– Inrap provides the scientific exploitation of preventive archaeology operations and the dissemination of their results;
– Inrap contributes to education, cultural and scientific development

Inrap must be the engine of quality process necessary for our discipline approach.

This process is complex and cumbersome due mainly to 2 features: – actors and structures spreading – practices rooting.

Our activity covers the entire country. Inrap traces its organization roots in Afan which did not have developed scientific and technical directions that can federate its action.

The activity is mainly organized in 9 interregional directions, based on 41 permanent archaeological research Centres. Quality approach develops in 4 steps: archaeological sites, archaeological research Centres, interregional directions, National Management. In research Centres and fields, approaches are very different from each other. They are mainly based on individual sensitivities and initiatives. Those approaches are sometimes valued, mainly when they are integrated into an improvement project developed by an interregional direction. But basically, quality control is within the purview of Inrap presidency and general management.

For archaeological operations, three work streams are mobilized: administrative, technical and scientific.

The quality approach to the administrative aspects is hardly different than any public institution is required to do. We will not address these issues here. For technical aspects, we were inspired by common ones developed at any civil engineering worksite.

Science is the most complex and the most sensitive.

Despite all the theoretical work that preceded and accompanied the archaeology practice today, the urgency 'to do' make us believe that the assessment of a 'know how' was nearly enough in terms of quality control.

An elementary process approach leads to split this 'expertise' in:

- what can't be explained that is due to an archaeological knowledge and which can only be transmitted through skills and learning.
- This knowledge does not lend itself to quality control, except in the form of subjective assessments. It's nurtured with curiosity and invention and it's essential. It helps to change the archaeological doctrine;
- what could be the basis of 'state of the art' in archaeology. This would be formalized, explained and agreed. Thus, it would contribute to a general repository required by a relevant quality control.

Beyond the question of the legitimacy of these rules (and that of who assumes it), those rules must be fully applied and the procedure must be checked regularly. If we all agree on the need to work on representative and reliable data, it is less exciting to have to apply common rules and in addition having to 'suffer' controls. The introduction of a real quality control requires a radical culture change.

Inrap has no quality management system (QMS), it has no certification according to ISO 9001. However, Inrap Scientific and Technical direction is undertaken in:

- the overall analysis of problems and the identification of issues
- the definition of priorities depending on various parameters not always scientific
- then the more detailed analysis of priorities
- the search for solutions, temporary or more lasting
- the recommendations or obligations: create a process repository
- the definition of new skills
- the phasing of an appropriate organization
- the phasing of reasonable quality controls

Examples

Technical aspects

The technical aspects of projects are probably the most advanced sector in our quality area. In these so-called technical aspects, we first integrate Health and Safety conditions. Agents are mandated to perform independent checks on their archaeological excavations to ensure compliance with the health and safety rules. This control can bring the prohibition of certain practices, and the obligation to take the necessary corrective measures. Training courses for archaeologists are required in this specific area. For many archaeologists, this training is the first professional entry into the world of civil engineering projects. The technical organization of the archaeological sites was originally based on too much improvisation.

In 2006, an internal Inrap seminar on the mechanization of excavation laid the foundation for a more professional approach to our field work.

A works supervisor has been integrated into Inrap's Scientific and Technical Direction, he develops this process. As with any civil engineering project, all necessary steps for an archaeological operation must be designed, organized, directed and linked to each other. These approaches are technical studies prior to excavation.

It was first necessary to establish a common vocabulary (mechanical supplies, equipment, procedures) shared by our providers. This work permit to establish a national public contract really adapted to our needs and obligations. The adaptation of existing repositories has produced a global documentation for Inrap agents, especially after dedicated training sessions. It was necessary to develop a new business for agents trained in technical aspects. A network of skills is now focused on maintaining exchanges and expertises. These skills and this organization allow gradual introduction of quality control for all technical aspects in the archaeological field.

Many efforts are made to continually improve our field activity. The objective is to optimize the quality of archaeological operations but also the organization and the expertise capacity of Inrap. The main objective is to precisely define the duties of each participant and highlight problems or malfunctions that can be corrected and cropped.

For optimum efficiency of technical studies, it is imperative to establish a minimum of procedures. These procedures are derived from for civil engineering projects common procedures (ISO 9000 family). We will not detail them but we retain the four usual major phases:

- the study
- the preparation
- the monitoring
- the final record

This last step is crucial and is itself a global quality control of technical aspects of the field and research work.

Intervention Projects

Since 2003, a new balance had to be struck between a specification necessarily more precise and the detailed and comprehensive field and research projects which frequently incorporates a technical brief. Projects have become records of dozens of pages.

The introduction of an internal quality control was held essential (necessary) to support this development. This control is applied to complex and / or major surveys and excavations and is implemented by the Scientific and Technical Direction.

Such expertise is used on:

- how to raise the issue and objectives based according to specification (Ministry of Culture specifications)?
- the correlation between means, methods and objectives developed into Inrap scientific intervention project in response to Ministry of Culture specifications
- the ease of reading and understanding the archaeological project

We have observed, after 3 years of work, a substantial improvement in our intervention projects.

Operation report

Work led to the development of a single template model report. This model improves the quality of presentation of archaeological reports. It also facilitates their identification. A simplified version in Word format can be used by any Inrap agent. In Design format is used by designers and graphic designers which provide quality control of those productions. Designers and graphic designers also provide the print quality control provided by an external service provider. The prints are also provided in digital format. This format enables archiving and on line publishing.

Regarding contents, a work is conducted for several years on the entire graphics chain, especially with the desire to further harmonize the performances.

Recommendations are made to designers and graphic designers. For example, rules were proposed that should contain a block plan, how this information should be represented. Rules are also proposed for the documentation produced on field. These rules may ultimately contribute to a graphical harmonized standard.

What is scientific quality control on field?

The act of searching transforms potential archives (remains) into interpreted scientific literature. A fundamental question is probably to inquire into the quality of this transformation:

- has the potential been identified? have archives been seen in their entirety and have they been properly evaluated?
- have the archaeological conditions been met on field? The examination of the report can't afford a full appreciation of the quality of the field research, including the adequacy of methodological and technical choices and means implemented.
- were the data recorded and the documentation relevant?

What 'compliance' can be defined in this case? And how to evaluate it?

In the process of excavation, the archaeological heritage is primarily a scientific heritage. It is the scientific analysis that makes sense. And this scientific dimension begins long before the first trowel shot. If quality controls must be put in place, they must first meet the requirement of researchers to generate and operate a reliable scientific data of known quality. But warn us against drifts, which would develop a minimum quality to become the standard quality.

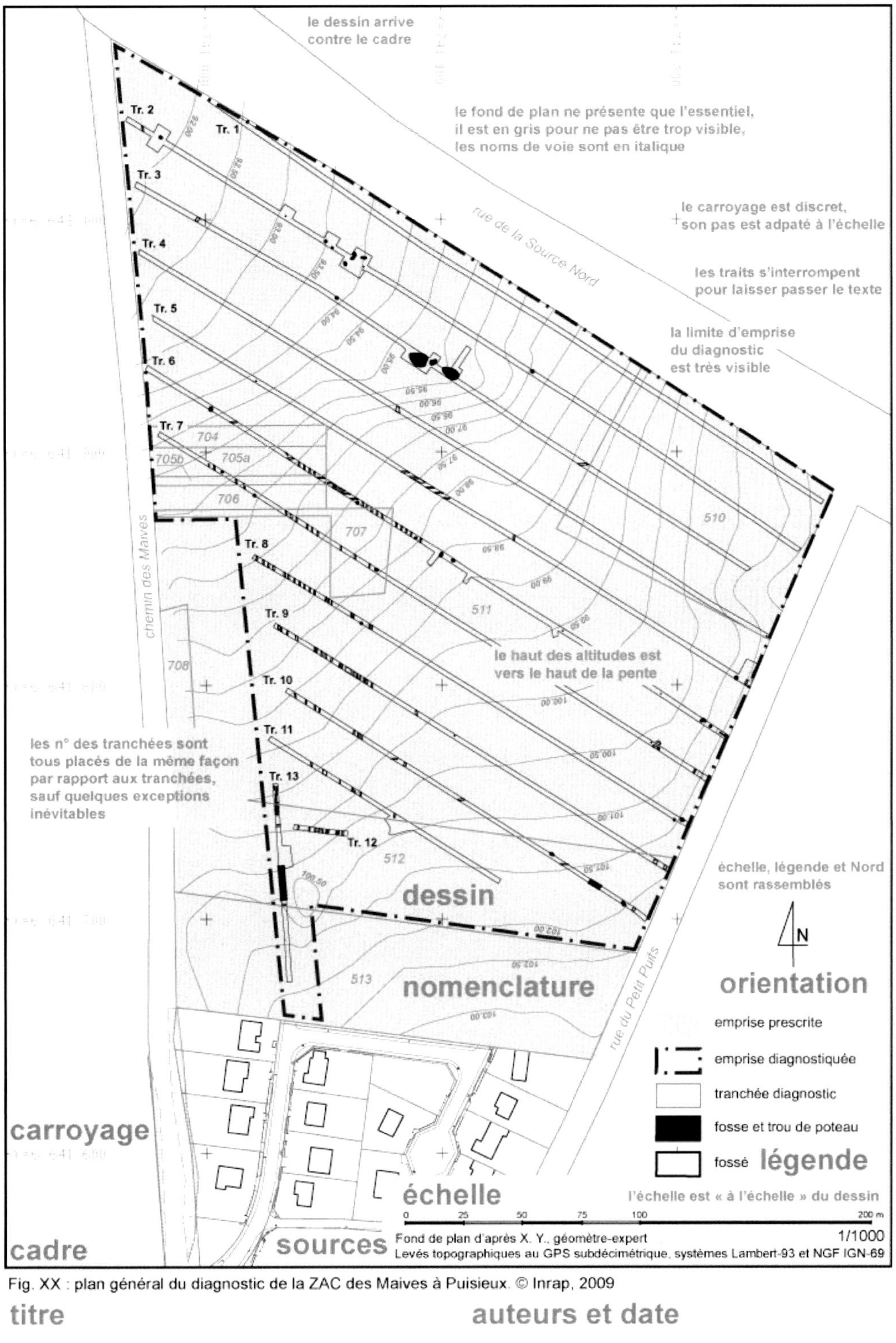

Figure 3. To define graphic chart is the necessary basis to all graphic work

Quality control in preventive archaeology in France: a review of the question

Pascal Depaepe
Inrap (National Institute for Preventive Archaeological Research, France), UMR 7164 CNRS and UISPP Commission 'Archaeological Heritage Policies and Management Structures'
pascal.depaepe@inrap.fr

Abstract
The state traditionally plays a central role in France and quality control in preventive archaeology is exclusively controlled by state services. On account of this, public and private operators have not, or have only slightly developed internal control systems for monitoring scientific, technical, societal and environmental quality (with the exception of Inrap). This article presents an overview of the problems encountered and proposes a number of solutions.

Résumé
La France est un pays dans lequel le rôle de l'état est traditionnellement fort. De ce fait, le contrôle qualité en archéologie préventive est l'apanage des services de l'état, et les opérateurs publics et privés, n'ont pas ou peu développé de systèmes internes de contrôle de la qualité scientifique, technique, sociétale et environnementale (à l'exception de l'Inrap).

Cet article dresse un état des problèmes rencontrés et propose quelques solutions.

Why apply a quality control to preventive archaeology?

Unlike 'academic' (or programmed) archaeology, preventive archaeology is both scientific and economic (in the broad sense of the term). It is clear that the scientific aspect of preventive archaeology must be assessed by the archaeological community on the basis of the analysis of scientific publications, congress presentations, etc., and in this respect, preventive archaeology is evaluated is the same way as any other scientific discipline. In addition, in France, the CIRA[1] (Commissions interrégionales de la recherche archéologique – see: Commission supérieure de codification, 2012, art. 545-16 and sq.), a system of commissions made up of specialists, inspects the results of archaeological operations.

Preventive archaeology is also an economic activity (the developer pays for the archaeological excavation) and takes place in a competitive context. The developer (the client) is supposed to look for the best value, like in any commercial transaction. But the difference between this context and standard transactions is that the archaeological excavation is an obligation and not a choice for the developer, who views the land as a plot for construction. In this way, the developer is not the end user of the product that he is paying for, as this product presents scientific and heritage interest and is aimed at researchers and the community in general. Therefore, the developer tries to keep archaeological costs as low as possible, without taking into account the quality of the intervention (Depaepe and Salas-Rossenbach, 2013; Van den Dries and Willems, 2007). This risk is taken into consideration by French law, which stipulates that the State (Ministry of Culture):

- sets out scientific specifications to guide the developer in choosing an archaeological operator,
- validates the project proposed by the operator,
- and ensures the scientific control of the archaeological operation.

[1] There is also the National Commission for Archaeological Research (CNRA), whose main role is to assess applications from operators, as well as to establish research programming in archaeology, although this latter aspect has not yet been completed (planned for September 2015).

The attribution of this state competence is intended to ensure the impartiality of the controls and the quality of the operations, which is all the more important given that the archaeological site is not renewable and that its destruction is irreversible and definitive. This monitoring is generally satisfactory, even though some errors or problems are unavoidable, generally on account of the lack of means allocated to the agents in charge of the control (see the work of the Commission of scientific, economic and social evaluation for preventive archaeology, Collective 2013), but sometimes due to external pressure for economic, or even political reasons.

However, state – Ministry of Culture monitoring only concerns strictly scientific activities, such as the aims of the operation and the methods and techniques used. No controls are undertaken for the other activities involved in the operation:

- Personnel management
- Security
- Compliance with environmental regulations
- Compliance with social standards (salaries, work conditions, etc.)

In theory, these aspects are monitored by the different organizations in charge, such as Work Inspection, the DRIRE,[2] etc. However, these organizations do not yet seem to consider preventive archaeology as one of their activities and these controls are rare, or even non-existent.

Therefore, some preventive archaeology operators have set up their own systems of quality control, referred to as 'management or quality supervision', as this is internal rather than external monitoring. The Inrap (Institut national de recherches archéologiques préventives), for example, has developed this topic extensively (Koehler, s.p., this volume).

Preventive archaeology procedures in France

Preventive archaeology procedures in France are rather complex, and the state plays a central role. This approach is in keeping with the French administrative tradition (Commission supérieure de codification, 2012; see Collart, 2012 for an accurate description of procedures).

Developers wishing to build new constructions must declare their intentions to the state, and the latter then monitors several aspects of the case: environment, urban planning, etc., including archaeology. The Ministry of Culture then evaluates the project with the regional services, in order to assess the possible consequences for archaeological heritage, and to decide whether or not to proceed with a preliminary study (the French term is 'diagnostic archéologique', or archaeological evaluation) to verify the presence of archaeological elements on the site chosen by the developer.

The archaeological evaluation is either carried out by Inrap, or by local authority services. These services must be certified by the Ministry of Culture to ensure the quality of work. The cost of the archaeological operation is covered by a tax: la Redevance d'Archéologie Préventive (RAP – Preventive Archaeology fee[3]). The tax is collected by the state for each development project: roads, building (factories, housing,...), airports, railway lines, etc. Ground exploitations such as quarries and gravel pits, etc. also have to pay this tax. A state-managed fund (le Fond National d'Archéologie Préventive – FNAP – National Preventive Archaeology Fund) centralizes the proceeds from the tax.

Resources are pooled in order to spread out the financial burden of diagnostics and to keep costs down. Each developer pays the tax, but this does not automatically involve a diagnostic. The latter is called for on the basis of scientific and heritage considerations.

[2] Direction régionale de la recherche, de l'industrie et de l'environnement (Regional Direction for research, industry and the environment).

[3] For a complete description of the RAP, see: http://vosdroits.service-public.fr/professionnels-entreprises/F22286.xhtml.

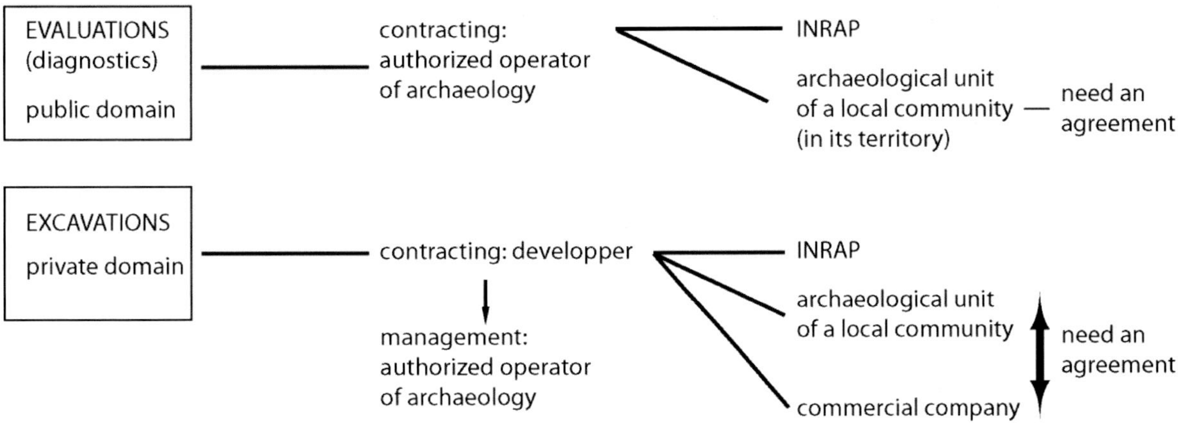

Figure 1. Principles of french preventive archaeology (from Collart 2012, modified)

Money from the FNAP is allocated to three types of actions:

- 70% is used to fund archaeological diagnostics and scientific research;
- 30% goes towards subsidizing developers whose projects are jeopardized by excavation costs, as well as towards financing individual and social housing.

If the diagnostic reveals the existence of an archaeological site, it must describe the extent, depth, age and characteristics of the site. Based on this, the state can decide whether or not an archaeological excavation is required and supplies the developer with the scientific requirements specification (SRS – figure 1).

The cost of the excavation is entirely paid by the developer (the polluter pays principle). The developer can call upon Inrap, local authorities or a commercial enterprise. However, the latter two must be certified by the Ministry of Culture in order to carry out excavations.

After the excavation, the report is transmitted to an independent scientific commission: the CIRA (cf. supra). The latter gauges the scientific value of the report and can ask for it to be completed or corrected.

Quality control in France

Quality control: a state affair

As stated above, quality control in France is a state affair. One of the main players is the Service Régional de l'Archéologie (SRA – regional archaeological service), an agency of the Ministry of Culture, working in conjunction with regional prefects, who depend upon the Ministry of Home Affairs. This hierarchical organization may account for some of the flaws in the management of sensitive issues, such as the absence of archaeological requirements for the site of the future Sivens dam, for example, even though the surface to be developed is extensive (40 hectares) and potentially archaeologically significant (Souchay, 2014).

Therefore, the SRA is at the core of preventive archaeology, both for prescribing and monitoring operations, as well as for writing up the scientific requirements specifications (see, among others, Catteddu *et al.*, 2012 – figure 2). As stated above, monitoring is generally satisfactory. However, decreases in state funding due to public policies of budgetary rigour have led to increasing difficulties in carrying out its tasks. Without prejudging the future, it t is clear that these constraints could

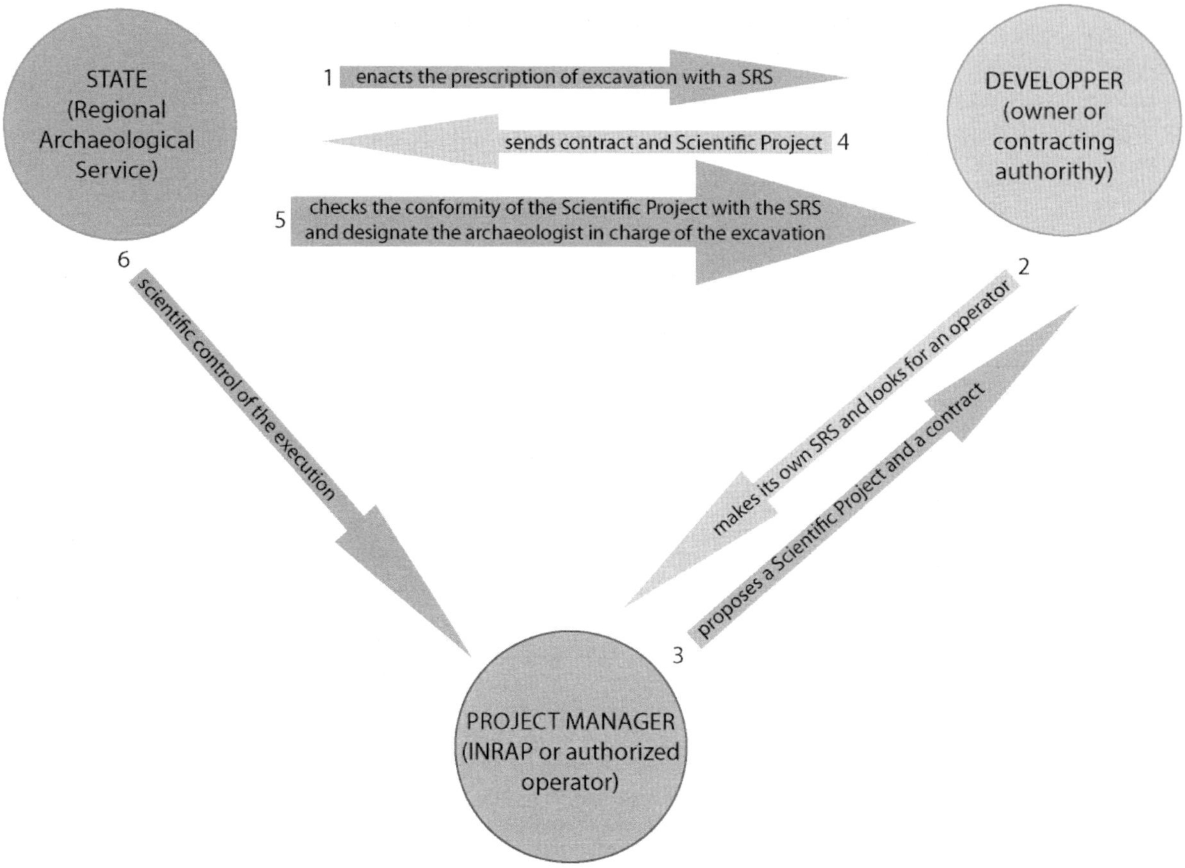

FIGURE 2. RULES OF EACH PARTNER BEFORE AND DURING A PREVENTIVE EXCAVATION (FROM COLLART 2012, MODIFIED)

result in more lax monitoring and may have a negative impact on future archaeological operations. Besides its daily work, the SRA can request a specific valuation from the regional CIRA, to help with monitoring.

A strong regulatory tradition

Traditionally, France has a strong regulatory tradition, like many other Latin countries. Unlike countries with Nordic and Protestant traditions (Germany, Scandinavia, the Netherlands, Great Britain), which are geared towards self-evaluation and peer control, France considers that control is part of the state domain, down to the last detail. It is beyond the scope of this paper to assess these notions of the role of the state, as this would extend outside the domain of archaeology. Here, we will limit out analysis to the consequences of this approach for preventive archaeology.

France has thus set out rather detailed regulations for preventive archaeology. After the law creating preventive archaeology was passed in 2001, several decrees, bylaws and ministerial circulars specified the application framework of this legislation. The law was then modified in 2003, and the regulations were reorganized in the Heritage Code, apart from bylaws and ministerial circulars.

The regulation of operations is described in these two strictly administrative, and not technical, articles. The more operational aspects are detailed in the bylaws. However, these bylaws[4] are still to a large extent a catalogue of the necessary elements and documents for the excavation report and not a technical description of the regulations. For example, the documents set out the scale of the maps

[4] Bylaws passed on 25/08/2004, 16/09/2004 and 27/09/2004.

to be supplied or the compulsory bibliographic rules. It would be useful if these bylaws referred to technical archaeological manuals defining the norms and minimum standards. Unfortunately, no such manuals exist!

Problems encountered and ways to improve them

Problems

There are many problems currently related to quality control in preventive archaeology. To sum up, we can say that they are inherent to a relatively recent discipline, still in the construction process. Moreover, preventive archaeology is still not considered to be a 'serious' activity by (public or private) authorities responsible for monitoring or management quality advice. Archaeology is often perceived as a Sunday activity, for retired teachers, eccentric scholars and young fanatics in search of treasure (from the Incas or Templars). In reality, preventive archaeology combines the restrictions of scientific research and civil engineering public earthworks, which make it a complex discipline requiring varied competencies. And thus considerable monitoring. It is significant that Inrap is currently the only organization with services and authorities specifically dedicated to management and quality control. This is the scientific, multi-disciplinary and multi-institutional council; the scientific and technical direction; as well as the regional authorities: hygiene and security committee, technical committee. These exist by regulation in commercial archaeological companies with more than 50 employees but companies rarely reach this scale (perhaps three in 2015, out of about 20). The same applies to regional authorities, although for the latter, the CHS are not dedicated to archaeology; they deal with all the local activities, in which archaeology only plays a minor role. The other operators have not installed internal control systems, and base their monitoring procedures on those carried out by state services. Establishing national standards would be a considerable step forward and in time, would no doubt simplify monitoring. The state services in charge of monitoring include those dedicated to heritage management (SRA, CIRA, CNRA), and those concerned with monitoring other aspects (DRIRE, Work inspection, etc.). For these latter authorities, archaeology is far from being a priority. This thus leads to a deficiency, or even a total absence of controls for non-archaeological aspects, such as work conditions, respecting environmental legislation, etc. As the promoter is the construction manager under French law, the latter should in theory deal with these issues. Yet, in most cases, the promoter is not interested in this or in the results of the archaeological operation.

As for the heritage management services, they have suffered for a long time from a lack of material and human resources. This is common knowledge, but few solutions have been put forward. The renewal of agents in these services is also an issue, as the high average age of employees in this sector[5] will lead to mass departures in the near future. Given the current policy of reducing employment in the public sector, it is legitimate to ask whether or not these agents will be replaced.

The scarcity of resources is also an issue for the CIRA and CNRA commissions. Some of these commissions contest the current method of appointment by the Ministry of Culture and wish to set up elections by peers. Here, we are concerned with the question of continuous control, after the attribution of the authorization to carry out a diagnostic and/or excavations. This authorization is based on a range of varied competencies but:

- Only strictly archaeological competencies are examined;
- The multiplication of operators has led to a high turnover of employees between structures and therefore the authorization can be granted on the basis of competencies that no longer exist.

This is a particularly important point given that most of the operators are small structures and only employ a few workers, and that they are considerably weakened if one of them leaves.

[5] In the SRA agents over 50 years old represent a total of 54.8%; those under 40 years old only make up 12.3% (2013 data, see (Collectif, 2013).

Several proposals to improve quality control

A commission met in 2012, at the request of the Ministry of Culture, and issued a white paper in 2013, in order to establish an overview of preventive archaeology in France and to suggest ways to improve it (Collectif, 2013). Proposals were made by this commission on scientific and regulatory aspects (which I will refer to here) in order to guarantee the quality of archaeological operations. However, two years after the publication of this report, no new measures have been implemented.[6] Yet, improvements could be made to the system without modifying the legislative framework of archaeology. Several of these are listed below, for discussion:

A) The SRA lacks resources and suffers from an ageing workforce. If agents from Inrap or from other local authorities were made available, this would enable the SRA to reinforce their analytic monitoring capacities, as these agents are familiar with fieldwork-related questions.

B) It is clear that preventive archaeology generates a considerable quantity of scientific data. Yet, the ministry in charge of research does not seem interested in this discipline. This absence of consideration is harmful for preventive archaeology as the latter relies solely on the Ministry of Culture, which is in charge of heritage and not scientific research, and thus by default it keeps preventive archaeology out of the scientific domain. Yet, given the mass of data produced, better organization between research carried out by the different players would represent considerable progress for our knowledge of the past.

In 2012, the Ministry of Research nonetheless launched an annual call for scientific projects specifically reserved for preventive archaeology. But the funds involved were ridiculously low: amounting to just 125,000 €, whereas the turnover in French preventive archaeology is over 200 M€.

C) In France, there is no evaluation system for archaeologists working in preventive archaeology. Their work is examined occasionally either by the CIRA (for reports of excavations and diagnostics), or by reading committees for scientific reviews (for articles). The implementation of a coherent and harmonized evaluation system would thus represent major progress and would enable the profession to gain official recognition on the basis of tangible elements common to all archaeologists.

D) Unlike in other countries (like the Netherlands, (see Willems and Brandt, 2004), there are no standards for archaeology in France. Yet, given the number of operators, this harmonization would be advantageous for establishing quality criteria and would facilitate the monitoring of operations. It would involve the setting up of a flexible system, leaving room for methodological innovation. However, it is important to recall that the excavation irremediably destroys the archaeological site and that monitoring remains one of the most effective ways of ensuring that this destruction takes place in accordance with the rules.

E) In many countries, archaeologists have merged into professional associations. This approach does not exist in France. Yet, the multiplicity of statuses[7] leads to various differences of opinion, and the merging of archaeologists into an association would enable them to weigh in more heavily on political choices and to gain recognition for the profession, independently of the type of employer.

Other changes are possible, but these would require legislative change:

A) French law gives regional prefects (and therefore the SRA linked to them) the power to designate the scientific leaders of archaeological preventive operations. This organization leads to diverse difficulties and it would be useful to review the advantages and disadvantages of such a system. One

[6] At the beginning of 2015, the Ministry of Culture asked a parliamentarian to establish a report on preventive archaeology. This is the 42nd report on preventive archaeology since 1976!

[7] At least 6 different statuses: state, university, CNRS, Inrap, local authorities, private enterprises.

possibility could be to grant the excavation authorization to a legal entity (the operator), who would then appoint the scientific leader (the prefect would retain a right of veto). The latter should be part of a list of authorized people (several scientific criteria are possible), coordinated by the CIRA and updated regularly.

B) The developer is currently in charge of the supervision of archaeological excavations. However, the general consensus among the scientific community is that the state should be responsible, as the developer does not have any vested interest in the archaeological operation, as this is not the product he is buying.

C) Many archaeologists would like to see preventive archaeology in the public system once again. In spite of certain statements, from a legal point of view, this is perfectly feasible (Demoule, 2013). It is just a question of political resolve… that no government appears to have, at least, not up until now. However, the integration of archaeologists working in France in the same institution would resolve many problems.

Conclusions

The quality approach in preventive archaeology in France is a fundamentally important subject, which is generally only marginally broached, with no coordination between the different players involved. However, there are different possibilities for better management, and some of these do not require legislative change. But they do require agreement among the different, divided players in the profession, and the consideration of preventive archaeology by political representatives, independently of any ideological or partisan approach.

References

Catteddu, I., Baillieu, M., Depaepe, P., Roffignon, A. (2012) – L'archéologie préventive en France : un service public original, *Post-Classical Archaeologies*, 2, p. 319-336.

Collart, J. L. (2012) – L'archéologie préventive en France: le cadre réglementaire et son application, In *Development-led archaeology in northwest Europe proceedings of a round table at the University of Leicester, 19th – 21st November 2009*, Oxford [u.a.], Oxbow Books, p. 56-99.

Collectif (2013) – *Livre blanc de l'archéologie préventive*, Ministère de la Culture et de la Communication, 2013 Consultable à http://www.culturecommunication.gouv.fr/Politiques-ministerielles/Archeologie/Livre_blanc.

Commission supérieure de codification (2012) – *Code du patrimoine: parties législative et réglementaire*, Paris, les Éd. des Journaux officiels, 2012.

Demoule, J. P. (2013) – A quoi sert l'état ?, http://www.jeanpauldemoule.com/a-quoi-sert-letat/.

Depaepe, P., Salas-Rossenbach, K. (2013) – Preventive archaeology in France, review and point of view, In *Twenty years after Malta preventive archaeology in Europe and in Italy*, Guermandi M. P., Salas-Rossenbach K., p. 129-136.

Van Den Dries, M., Willems, W. (2007) – Quality assurance in archaeology, the Dutch perspective, In *Quality management in archaeology*, Oxford, Oxbow, p. 50-65.

Koehler, A. (s.p.) (2014) – Quality management organisation in Inrap (France), In Depaepe P. & Engovatova A., *Management and use of science data from preventive archaeology: quality control*, XVIIe World Congress UISPP, Burgos, 2014.

Souchay, G. (2014) – Au Testet, l'Etat piétine la loi sur l'archéologie, *Reporterre, le quotidien de l'écologie*. http://www.reporterre.net/Au-Testet-l-Etat-pietine-la-loi.

Willems, W. J. H., Brandt, R. W. (2004) – *Dutch Archaeology Quality Standard*, Den Haag, (RIA-Report, 2004, 232 p.

Archaeology in Russia today – the system of scientific control over the quality of rescue archaeology work

Asya Engovatova
The Institute of Archaeology of the Russian Academy of Sciences,
Ul Dm Ulyanova 19. Moscow, 117036. Russia
engov@mail.ru

Abstract

In Russia, there are approximately 60,000 registered archaeological sites and over 1500 archaeological projects are undertaken annually. Rescue archaeology projects undertaken in Russia have risen significantly, now accounting for over 70% of all archaeological research in Russia. The principle recent trend is a sharp increase in the proportion of rescue archaeology projects undertaken by non-State companies. Since 2006 the number of projects undertaken by private companies has more than trebled. By 2012-2013 their share of the overall number of projects had risen to around 40%. The pace of change is largely due to Russia's taxation system. Economic reform has enabled tax-breaks stimulating the growth of non-State business. Yet State organisations (museums, universities, affiliates of the RAS) enjoy none of these tax breaks. The playing field is not level – making it more attractive for both the contractors and the clients of such works to use non-governmental agencies.

This situation raises the serious question of the scientific control of such works.

Résumé

En Russie, il ya environ 60,000 sites archéologiques connus et plus de 1500 projets archéologiques sont entreprises chaque année.

Les projets d'archéologie de sauvetage menés en Russie ont considérablement augmenté, représentant désormais plus de 70% de toutes les recherches archéologiques en Russie. La tendance récente est une forte augmentation de la proportion des projets d'archéologie de sauvetage menés par les entreprises non étatiques. Depuis 2006, le nombre de projets entrepris par des sociétés privées a plus que triplé. En 2012-2013 leur part du nombre total de projets est passé à environ 40%.

Le rythme du changement est largement dû au système d'imposition de la Russie. La réforme économique a permis des allègements fiscaux stimulant la croissance des entreprises privées. Malheureusement, les organismes d'État (musées, universités, sociétés affiliées de la RAS) ne jouissent d'aucun de ces avantages fiscaux. La concurrence est donc faussée, et ce système attrayant pour les aménageurs ce qui les pousse à utiliser les services des compagnies non gouvernementales.

Cette situation soulève la grave question du contrôle scientifique de ces travaux.

Human interest in materials found at ancient sites is a fundamental aspect of our consciousness – a part of our spiritual culture. Today it is archaeology which gives us our scientific understanding of huge periods of the history of mankind. Developments in recent years have made demanding standards possible when presenting scientific information, bringing to reality society's interest in a scientific interpretation of materials from the past. Archaeology is broadening its base – increasing the number of excavations, publications, and the numbers of archaeological sites placed on protection lists.

Over the past two decades the overall amount of archaeological research in Russia has increased exponentially – but many aspects of modern archaeological activity (including the rapid commercialization of archaeological work) make it even more vital that the role of scientific investigation during archaeological work is retained – particularly during rescue archaeology work.

Designated Sites of Archaeological Heritage make up a significant part of Russia's cultural heritage. There are now more than 146 thousand Cultural Heritage Listed Sites in Russia, and of these nearly 40% (around 58 thousand sites) are designated Archaeological Heritage sites (including monuments and sightseeing locations). In a number of Russian Regions, more than 80% of protected Cultural Heritage Sites are archaeological locations – in the Republic of Khakhassia, the Khanty-Mansiysk Autonomous Region (Yugra), the Republic of Tuva, the Altai Republic, Rostov Region, and many others. However, there are also many areas where the number of archaeological sites listed as Cultural Heritage Sites is very low. Lists maintained by regional protection bodies number more than 75,000 listed sites of archaeological interest (a lower category than archaeological locations, but still protected from destruction in law). This means that the overall number of archaeological sites throughout Russia can be numbered at over 133,000 (see figure 1).

The explanation for this disproportion in the regional distribution of Russia's archaeological sites lies principally in the haphazard pace at which archaeological studies have been carried out in different areas – allied to the uneven pace at which the different regions have allocated Listed Status to such sites and put them onto the State Register. Today's picture of accumulated archaeological material cannot be said to reflect the actual histories or development of society in these areas. The uneven degree to which archaeological work has been conducted in these areas can be traced to a number of factors – which include the existence (or absence) of research centers with experienced staff, and additionally the geographical accessibility of the terrain in many cases. A significant role is played by the level of activity and professional competence of regional bodies set up for the State protection of heritage sites – and how far their work extends to sites of archaeological significance. Statistical data permits us to draw up lists of 'regional leaders' with good operational practice in caring for cultural heritage sites – where archaeological sites have been correctly placed on the State Register (recognized as such, and placed on the Register with the correct status) and which display an ongoing high level of archaeological fieldwork being conducted (see figure 2).

Across the whole of Russia, the number of archaeological operations conducted annually has numbered more than 1500 sites in recent years. Included in this overall total of archaeological

Figure 1. Estimated number of archaeological sites in Russia

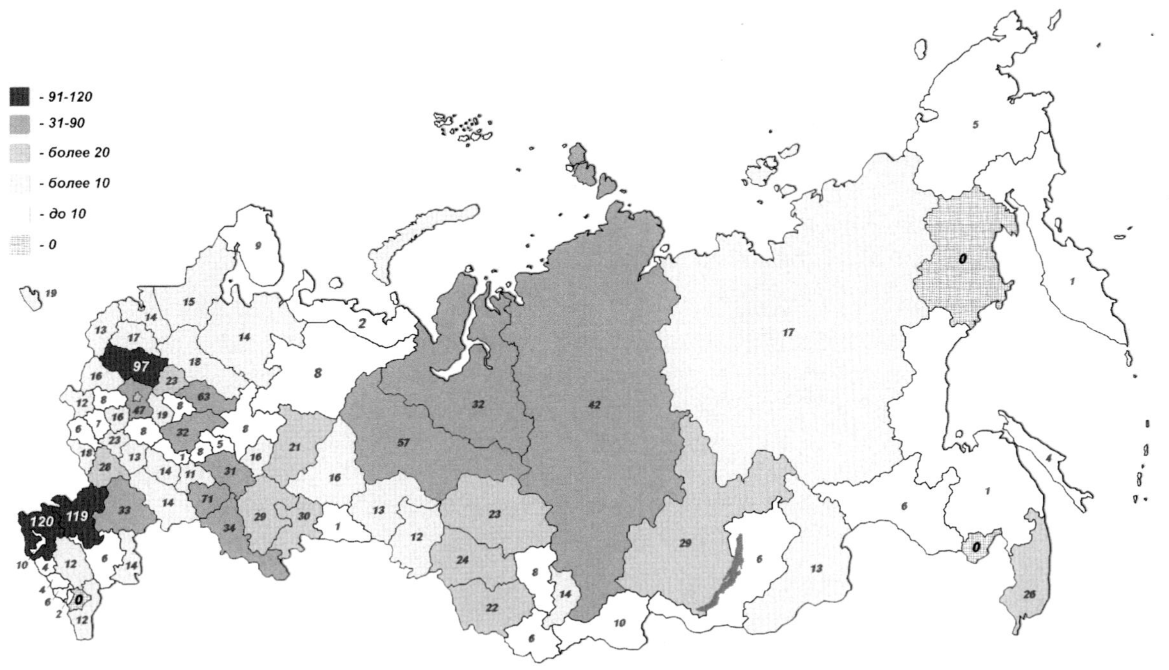

Figure 2. Number of archaeological fieldwork in Russia in 2014

operations is a continuously growing percentage of rescue archaeology sites. The rise in this kind of work is steep, and today such sites constitute more than 70% of the overall number of sites. A growing tendency to be clearly seen in the statistics for the past two decades is that of work being undertaken by non-State (ie private) companies on archaeological sites. Since 2006 the extent of studies undertaken by private companies has more than tripled. In the 2012-2014 period, such work accounted for approximately 40% of the overall total.

This phenomenon has roots in the prevailing taxation system in Russia. The liberalization of the post-Soviet Russian economy resulted in laws which promote the development of non-state, private small businesses. However, government organizations (including museums, universities, institutions of the Russian Academy of Sciences, and others) who undertake the self-same work are unable to benefit from these same tax breaks enjoyed by private companies. Moreover, these tax breaks apply not only to the private companies who undertake the work, but similarly to the clients for whom the works are done. This uneven playing field imperils the standards of scientific research which are an obligatory part of archaeological studies.

It should be noted that archaeological works undertaken in Russia are permitted only with the issue of license to carry them out (the so-called Open List permit). An Open List can only be issued by the Ministry of Culture of the Russian Federation. The initial stage of control of archaeological work comprises the consideration of the Application for such a permit, and the conditions for its issue. (These are regulated by the 'Rules for the issue, provision, or cancellation of permits (Open Lists) for carrying out work on the identification and study of sites of archaeological heritage' as laid in the Federal Law N° 127 of 20th February 2014).

The next stage is sending a request to the Scientific Committee for Fieldwork at the Russian Academy of Sciences (which is based at the Institute of Archaeology of the RAS). Verification will be conducted concerning the suitability of documents which have been submitted by the applicant, the level of archaeological work which has been done, the research methods, and the professional qualifications held by the applicants. Permits will only be issued to qualified archaeologists with appropriate professional education and a due level of fieldwork experience (or participation in fieldwork, for first-time applicants). Once fieldwork is completed, there's an obligatory condition to lodge a Scientific Report of the results with the Scientific Committee for Fieldwork – to evaluate its conformity with the norms of such research, the methods deployed during the archaeological fieldwork, and the correctness of the Report's presentation. An unsatisfactory evaluation by the Committee can result in the denial of future applications for Open List permits. Open List permits are similarly denied to researchers who have failed to deliver due Scientific Reports for previous archaeological fieldwork.

The system for the scientific regulation of archaeological fieldwork in Russia was first developed in the previous century. Throughout Russia – and the USSR, for the period of its existence – rules have applied for 150 years governing the unified approach with respect to researching archaeological sites, methods of recording findings, and the format of the obligatory Scientific Report. The methodological regulations were developed by the Institute of Archaeology of the Russian Academy of Sciences. The research methods similarly govern the sphere of rescue archaeology. There are no 'quick fixes' or 'short cuts' permitted in rescue archaeology – so that the level of scientific research is not compromised. Although there have been attempts in recent years to bring in a system governing observation as a separate genre of work, it has not been accepted except in specific cases where the ground of an archaeological site has been damaged.

This means that the Russian Academy of Sciences retains control of the quality of all archaeological studies undertaken in Russia, thus ensuring the quality of such work on behalf of the Ministry of Culture of the Russian Federation. This situation is codified in the legislation of the Russian Federation under Law No 245-F3, of 23rd July 2013. It's a strong advantage that currently in Russia the system of rescue archaeology has had a strong scientific component for the past two centuries. In the nineteenth century, even when matters were controlled by a market economy, the standing of academic institutions was similarly high. On a graph showing the numbers of rescue archaeology projects over recent years, it can be clearly seen that such institutions carried out approximately one quarter of all such studies (cf Engovatova 2012 pp141-150). A further major advantage is that rescue archaeology in Russia retains its close links with academic science.

Over the last twenty years in Russia the share of archaeological fieldwork undertaken for purely scientific reasons and for fundamental research has declined. In recent years such fieldwork has comprised only 20% of the overall total. The primary funding for such research has come from RGNF (the Russian Humanitarian Science Foundation) and the RFFI (the Russian Fund for Fundamental Research); from Russian Academy of Science programs. Over recent years funding has also been provided by local financing from specific regions concerned (e.g. Tatarstan, Krasnodar Province and others) where regional budgeting is provided for such research. In fact, the last 20 years have witnessed a continuous growth in the amount of rescue archaeology fieldwork. The cause of pre-emptive intervention and priority study of sites – which may subsequently be lost forever due to construction projects – is one of the imperatives driving the strategy of archaeological fieldwork around the world. Nevertheless, it should not be forgotten that large-scale long-term fieldwork research projects have always been the primary driver of the development of scientific methods in archaeology – yet today, the number of such projects in Russia stands at a critical minimum.

Despite this, over recent decades Russia has approached the numbers of organized rescue archaeology projects typical in Western European countries, when expressed as a percentage total of all archaeological research. To give one example: in 1984, 70% of all archaeological work carried out in Russia was financed from governmental budgets. This figure for 2009 was just 26%. This trend is caused, in one part, by cuts in state support for basic research in humanitarian science – and on other, with the construction boom of recent decades, and the consequential rise in archaeological projects caused by this boom.

The legal obligation to make a Scientific Report to the Scientific Council for Fieldwork – for subsequent addition to the Russian Archive Foundation – makes all information obtained during studies and fieldwork available to the scientific community. In our opinion a reform of this system is needed which would make electronic publication of these reports compulsory, so that they were accessible to the scientific community, subject to appropriate copyright protection.

There has been a recent shift in archaeology's place in the system of human knowledge, and recent years have seen the humanitarian sciences take up a new position. If there is some kind of modern-world crisis of trust in the science of archaeology, then the discipline must reclaim its position in the system of scientific knowledge, and prove that society needs it. There is a special situation in Russia in this regard. In Russia, archaeology is responsible for the creation and continuous updating of the picture of human society's development – in a vast country, and down a long and winding time-line. This places a great responsibility on archaeology – to place the historic sites of Russia's ancient and medieval culture in their rightful place in world history, so that they assume their full role in the global world view. The groundbreaking achievements Russian archaeology has made in recent decades haven't truly entered the consciousness of Russian society, and their adoption in studies of history has been a painfully slow trickle. These achievements are quickly forgotten against the torrent of other news. Archaeology is expected to come up with more and more short-term sensations to slot into television schedules – with an ever-decreasing interest in deep scientific exploration of historical processes.

Archaeology in Russia reflects the deep swings going on in public consciousness – and these swings are all materializing in the practice, legislation, and culture. This is, in fact, the watchword – modern society looks at archaeology as not just a science, but as a significant and important part of world culture.

References

Engovatova, A. V. (2012) – Rescue Archaeology in Russia (published to mark the 40th anniversary of the Department of Protected Excavations of the Institute of Archaeology of the Russian Academy of Science) // RA 2012 No 4 pp 141-150.

Trois cas de prospections relatifs à des diagnostics archéologiques en Côte d'Ivoire (2008-2010): les entreprises d'extraction minière levier pour un nouvel ordre archéologique en Côte d'Ivoire?

Kouassi Kouakou Siméon

Archéologue enseignant-chercheur, Département d'Archéologie de l'Institut des Sciences, Anthropologiques de Développement (ISAD), Université Félix Houphouët-Boigny
kksimeon@yahoo.fr

François Guédé Yiodé

Archéologue, Institut d'Histoire d'Art et d'Archéologie Africains (IHAAA)/ Université Félix Houphouët-Boigny / Cocody-Abidjan – Côte d'Ivoire
gbeuyerebodigbeu@yahoo.fr

Résumé

L'archéologie préventive n'est pas encore appliquée mais commence à être pensée en Côte d'Ivoire. En témoigne la réceptivité, croissante, des autorités chargées des prescriptions des Etudes d'Impact Environnemental et Social de l'Agence Nationale de l'Environnement et du Bureau National d'Etudes Techniques et de Développement. Ce, selon les directives opérationnelles des bailleurs de fonds. Ces prospections voulues, par des miniers, en montrant l'importance des sites et vestiges soulignent l'opportunité de telles initiatives pour la recherche et l'enrichissement des fonds des musées.

Mots-clés

Côte d'Ivoire, Archéologie préventive, Vestiges archéologiques, Etudes d'Impact Environnemental et Social, Directives opérationnelles des bailleurs de fonds

Abstract

In Ivory Coast, preventive archaeology is not used so far. But today people are thinking about its use. This is seen through the increasing receptiveness of the authorities in charge of the prescription of Social and Environmental Impact Studies. According to the operational directives of financial backers such as the World Bank. These results sponsored by some mining firms show the opportunity such initiatives grant to research and the country museum fund enrichment.

Key-words

Ivory Coast, Preventive archaeology, Artefacts, Social and Environmental Impact Studies, Operational directives of financial backers

Introduction

Les trois missions de diagnostics archéologiques qui constituent la trame de notre travail se sont déroulées:

- Du 17 au 23 mai 2008 à Mbengué (Nord Côte d'Ivoire) sur le permis de la Société Rangold;
- Du 22 mai au 1er juin 2010 sur un permis de la société Occidental Gold dans la préfecture de Tengrela (Nord Côte d'Ivoire);
- Du 16 au 22 juin 2010 à Hiré (Centre-ouest Côte d'Ivoire) pour LGL, attributaire d'un permis d'exploitation minière.

Pour l'historique, les premières formes de collaboration entre archéologiques et autres domaines de recherche tournées vers la terre, notamment les géologues de la Société pour le Développement Minier de la Côte d'Ivoire (SODEMI), datent de 1970 à 1980. Les rapports d'études mis alors à la disposition des archéologues permirent d'étudier les amas coquilliers et des sites paléolithiques à Anyama et à Bingerville à l'est et à l'ouest d'Abidjan. Les résultats des prospections dans le cadre des diagnostics archéologiques effectués sur les trois sites mentionnés d'entrée, ont la spécificité de faire participer les archéologues à des recherches qui précèdent l'exploitation de mines d'or. Ce faisant, ils nous plongent dans l'esprit de ce qu'il est convenu d'appeler Archéologie préventive. Quelle importance revêt ces premières recherches et comment peuvent-elles contribuer à l'instauration d'un nouvel ordre archéologique en Côte d'Ivoire? Pour répondre à ces préoccupations nous montrons les conditions d'exécution desdits diagnostics, la méthode de travail et les sites et vestiges mis au jour.

Les conditions d'exécution des diagnostics

L'archéologie préventive implique un diagnostic et des fouilles. Pour nous en tenir au diagnostic, il consiste à analyser le terrain à aménager en vue de mesurer sa richesse en vestiges archéologiques avant les travaux. Il permet par des sondages archéologiques à circonscrire l'importance des artefacts. On a alors recours à : la prescription, la préparation de l'intervention sur le terrain, la mise en place d'une équipe, la mobilisation des moyens techniques et la vulgarisation des informations sur les vestiges mis au jour dans le secteur, l'intervention par sondages pour apprécier l'importance des vestiges et de leur enfouissement. Ainsi, si le diagnostic est négatif l'aménageur peut démarrer son travail; lorsqu'il est positif et l'intérêt scientifique des vestiges est moindre ou qu'ils sont mal conservés, l'aménageur est autorisé à mettre en valeur son terrain ; lorsqu'il est positif avec un intérêt scientifique certain et des vestiges bien conservés la fouille est prescrite et lorsqu'il révèle des vestiges exceptionnels, on demande à l'aménageur de les intégrer dans son projet (Démoule 2002 ; Jockey 1998).

Dans le cas présent, la loi n'existant pas et celle existante (loi n°87-806 du 28 juillet 1987 portant protection du patrimoine culturel' de Côte d'Ivoire) ne faisant pas obligation à l'aménageur de passer par l'étape de l'archéologie préventive, le sort de cette opération dépend du seul vouloir de ce dernier. Pour les diagnostics archéologiques de Mbengué, Tengrela et Hiré (Cf. Figure 1), c'est par l'intermédiaire de cabinets d'études en l'occurrence, CECAF international à Abidjan, que ces études ont eu lieu.

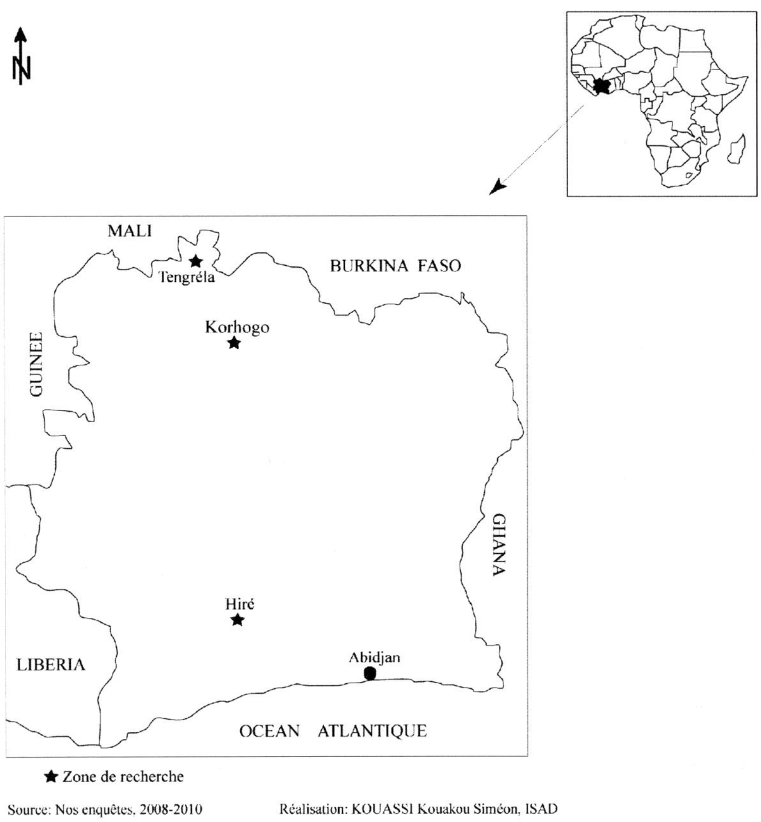

FIGURE 1. ZONE DE RECHERCHE

Dans la pratique, cette structure privée a requis, pour les comptes des clients Rangold, Occidental Gold et LGL attributaires de permis d'exploitations minières octroyé par le Gouvernement ivoirien, l'expertise d'archéologues locaux. Les tâches assignées aux missions consistaient à : effectuer une prospection itinérante des domaines miniers, dresser une carte de prospection représentant les différents sites découverts, interpréter les résultats obtenus, faire des recommandations pertinentes pour la protection du patrimoine mis en évidence.

L'objectif dans chaque cas, était d'exécuter d'étudier la voie d'acheminement du minerai aurifère, des aires d'exploitation et de stockage aux usines de Tongon à Mbengué, Sissigué à Tengrela et de Bonikro à Hiré. Les entreprises ont agi en respect des directives des bailleurs de fonds, comme la Banque mondiale. Celles-ci mettent un point d'honneur sur le fait que l'évaluation environnementale ne peut exclure le patrimoine culturel. En conditionnant tout financement de projet au respect desdites directives elles réaffirment le fait que l'identité et la culture des populations autochtones sont indissociables de leurs territoires (Manuel opérationnel de la Banque Mondiale, 2005; Banque Mondiale, n.d; Société Financière Internationale octobre 1998). Nous avons là un cas de jurisprudence qui peut aider à faire asseoir l'archéologie préventive. Si l'archéologie classique n'a pas toujours donné les moyens aux africains de s'exprimer convenablement, il est indéniable que l'archéologie préventive qui se présente comme une seconde chance, ne leur échappe pas. Une approche du terrain bien à propos a été adoptée.

La méthode de travail

A l'aide d'u Pick Up Toyota de type 4 x 4 mis à la disposition par CECAF International et les clients Rangold, Occidental Gold et LGL, les chercheurs se déplaçaient chaque jour, dans le domaine minier, pour les investigations. En plus des cartes et des coordonnées de base des tracés à observer (figure 2), les chercheurs collaboraient avec les populations locales.

C'est un gage de succès parce que par expérience, il est avéré que ces populations connaissent mieux leur environnement de vie. Beaucoup de réalités archéologiques leur sont connus du fait des activités

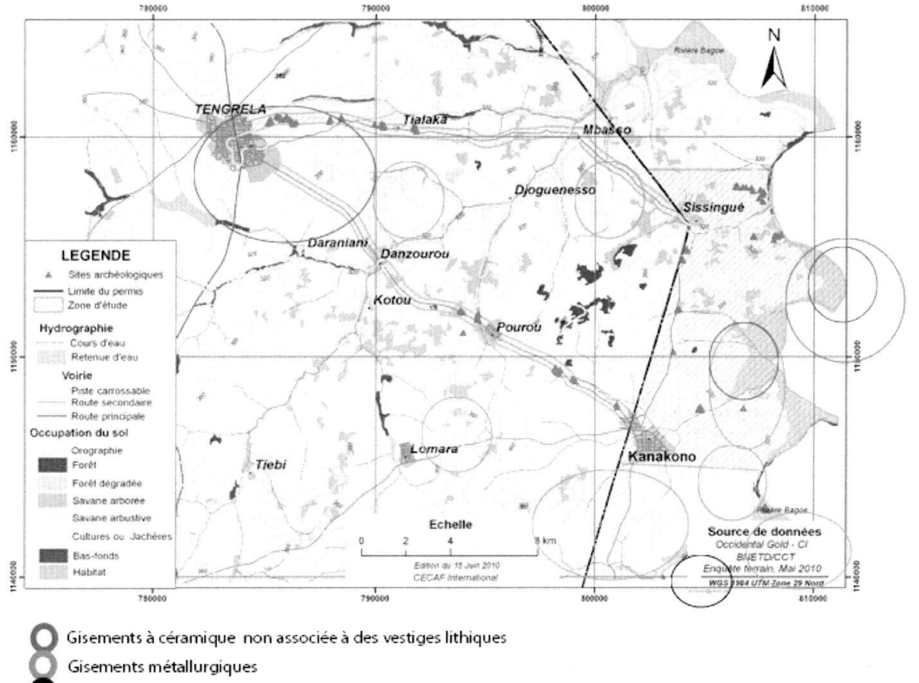

Figure 2. Exemple de carte des points de prelevements des vestiges archeologiques (Tengrela)

agricoles et de chasse auxquelles elles demeurent attachées, dès lors qu'elles en sont sensibilisées et instruites. A ce sujet un guide est recruté pour servir de traducteurs en langue locale. Il lui revenait de transmettre, aux populations réunies chez le chef de chaque village entouré de sa notabilité, les préoccupations des chercheurs.

Cette méthode a été déterminante pour la suite des missions. Au terme de ces rendez-vous, les dignitaires désignaient trois à quatre guides ayant une maîtrise sérieuse des secteurs à visiter pour répondre aux attentes. Le troisième appui stratégique de la méthode était le GPS.

Il servait à localiser les différents points observés. En outre, une boussole était utilisée pour lire les pendages et la direction des pentes des affleurements. Les prises de vues ont été effectuées à l'aide d'un appareil photographique numérique.

Les sites et vestiges mis au jour pouvant être sauvegardé

Les sites et vestiges découverts, et qui peuvent faire l'objet de conservation, sont représentatifs des différents âges de l'occupation humaine (figure 3). Les résultats obtenus, sont présentés par sites et par ordre chronologique des travaux effectués.

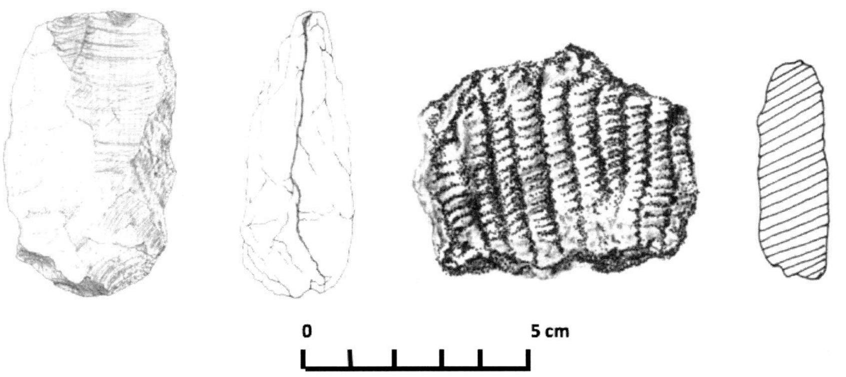

FIGURE 3. EXEMPLE D'HACHEREAU ET CERAMIQUE DE MBENGUE

Les recherches de Mbengué

Deux zones autour de l'exploration minière de Tongon qui s'étendent à l'Ouest et à l'Est permettent de présenter les prospections sur ce permis minier. Au total, sur 42 sites archéologiques repérés, on distingue à l'ouest, 30 sites dont 5 relèvent exclusivement du paléolithique, 8 gisements du néolithique, 6 constituent un mélange de vestiges paléolithiques et néolithiques, 11 sites métallurgiques. A l'Est, on dénombre 12 sites dont 3 du néolithique, 3 constitués d'un mélange de vestiges paléolithiques et néolithiques, 2 mésolithiques et 2 métallurgiques. A cela s'ajoute des sites divers.

Les sites paléolithiques

Les sites paléolithiques, sont regroupés dans la partie Ouest de Tongon. Une dizaine d'objets à été observé en association avec des vestiges néolithiques à trois endroits à l'Est de Tongon. On dénombre 50 pièces dont 15 proviennent des sites où l'outillage de ce type est mélangé avec celui du néolithique. On note la présence de séries lithiques appartenant à différentes époques. A Kabolô par exemple, les nucléi, très peu identifiés se repartissent en nucléi de type Middle Stone Age (MSA) (2 pièces), des formes prismatiques de même qu'à Katalaô où ont été récolté des bifaces de type acheuléen en association avec des pics sangoens comme à la Bété à Anyama et Gouabouo à Soubré (Guédé 2000; Guédé 2002). Par contre à Timblan, à Kronanliô et enfin à Djiô l'on distingue trois (03) types de complexes industriels:

- L'acheuléen caractérisé par la présence de bifaces amygdaloïdes et cordiforme;
- Le MSA par les formes limaçoïdes, les éclats en enlèvement centripète;
- Le paléolithique tardif reposant sur les formes prismatiques.

En outre, l'abondance, sur ces sites (Timblan, Kronanhiô) de déchets importants de taille permettent de dire qu'ils sont des ateliers. La matière première est constituée de granite à biotite, quartz à Kronanhiô et Timblan.

Les sites mésolithiques

Les sites mésolithiques sont au nombre de deux et localisés dans la zone de Tellings Dam, sur le flanc Ouest du forage TGWO4. Seulement 20 microlithes et éclats de taille on été collectés.

Les sites néolithiques

Les sites néolithiques sont présents de part et d'autre de Tongon, mais on les observe beaucoup plus à l'Ouest: huit sites contre trois à l'Est. Les industries néolithiques comportent 73 vestiges dont 32 haches taillées, 07 formes bifaciales de dimensions variables (10 cm à 21 cm), 03 pics, 05 fragments, 02 rabots, 01 meule et 18 tessons de céramique le tout confectionné sur des plaquettes et des éclats de dolérite. Les haches taillées restent le fossile directeur. Les séries présentées se caractérisent par un tranchant obtenu par percussion. Aucune hache polie n'a été observée.

Les sites métallurgiques

Les sites métallurgiques se situent aussi bien à l'Ouest qu'à l'Est de Tongon. Ils sont plus présents dans la partie ouest et se composent, dans leur ensemble, de vanneries, de teintureries, d'exploitation d'argile, de zones d'extraction de minerai de fer et de fonderies.

Teinturerie

Près de Poungbè, dans la direction Sud-ouest (secteur Kabè), a été observé un atelier de production de teinture. Il s'agit de petits trous circulaires de diamètre variable (20-50 cm) et de profondeur estimée à 20-50 cm, creusés dans la cuirasse latéritique de 100 m x 50 m de superficie. Dans ces trous, les artisans écrasaient une liane dite « **gala** » à l'aide des pilons pour obtenir la poudre qui entrait, plus tard, dans la composition de la teinture en la mélangeant à de l'eau.

Les points d'extraction d'argile

Il s'agit d'une zone d'emprunt d'argile. Les femmes y viennent s'approvisionner en matière première pour la fabrication des récipients en céramique, selon leurs besoins. Cette source d'approvisionnement est au Sud-est de Poungbè à 1,5 km environ, dudit lieu, dans une saprolite de roches volcaniques.

Les zones d'extractions du minerai de fer

On distingue deux zones d'extractions du minerai de fer dont l'une est située dans la montagne-refuge (Nord-ouest de Poungbè) et la deuxième – Solo – à l'Est des travaux miniers, près de Badeni. Dans la première zone, on observe près de Timblan, au sommet de la colline-refuge, une centaine de trous. Ils ont pour dimensions 75 cm à 100 cm environ, de diamètre sur une profondeur de 2 à 3 m et se rejoignent par des galeries souterraines. Ils sont creusés dans la cuirasse latéritique pour l'extraction du minerai de fer.

Les zones de réductions du minerai de fer

La cinquième série se rattachant aux sites métallurgiques s'identifie aux zones de réductions du minerai (figure 4) de fer qui occupent de grandes aires:

Figure 4A. (© Guédé Yiodé) e 4B. (© Kouassi Kouakou Siméon).
Fourneau et scories de fer de Nawavogo (Dokelevogo)

1. Dans le secteur de Kadjolô, Sud-ouest de Tongon, sur la pente Ouest d'une colline, où
2. D'importants dépôts de scories de fer sont encore observables sur une aire d'environ 200 m x 50 m. Le dépôt de scories est haut de 2,5 m et long de 50 m. Les restes de fourneaux (25 pièces) ont une hauteur d'environ 1,5 m et un diamètre de 92 cm;
3. Le second point, non loin du village de Nawavogo (Dokélévogo) a une extension au-delà de la route qui relie Tongon à celle de Korhogo. On y dénombre une dizaine de fourneaux du même type que ceux de Kadjolô.

Les autres sites

Les autres sites sont constitués d'un ensemble de lieux sacrés liés à des cultes d'adoration. Ils se situent autour de Tongon (dans la zone minière) et de Poungbè. En outre, on retiendra l'existence des rivières sacrées (Solo, près de la rivière Badeni et Djiô, où on adore les crocodiles du Bandama) et des forêts sacrées (forêt sacrée de Tchoro). On peut dire à l'issue de ces recherches que les résultats obtenus restent une base pour orienter des recherches plus approfondies. Il s'agit de:

1. La protection des zones de réduction, de teinturerie, des lieux cultuels et des zones;
2. D'extraction du minerai de fer. Les travaux à réaliser à cette fin sont la cartographie du secteur, la restauration des vestiges conservés in situ et la construction d'un bâtiment administratif;
3. La prolongation de la mission devant permettre de continuer la reconnaissance sur les Tellings-Dam, Dam option 1 et Dam option 2, secteur de Loa et de Poungbè. Car les informations sur ces sites sont insuffisantes et nécessitent des travaux additionnels pouvant durer 5 à 10 jours. En effet, c'est seulement dans les zones d'épandages qu'ont été récolté des vestiges d'âge mésolithique. La poursuite des travaux de reconnaissance s'étendra alors aux collines environnantes des secteurs cités plus haut. A cet effet on aura la latitude de prendre une décision objective concernant la zone des infrastructures minières projetées;
4. Une étude complémentaire en phase II pour une meilleure observation.

Les travaux complémentaires consisteront à mettre en œuvre une grille de layons espacés de 50 m, 100 m ou 200 m de longs selon les cas, pour un ratissage systématique, des sondages et une campagne de fouilles pour une chasse des vestiges en profondeur. La zone de Tengrela a livré des sites et vestiges relativement intéressants.

Les investigations de la préfecture de Tengrela

Les recherches dans la préfecture de Tengrela ont touché tous les types d'environnements d'intérêt archéologique. Sont mis en évidence quatre secteurs, dans le permis minier ayant fait l'objet des investigations. On peut y distinguer:

1. L'axe routier Nord: Tengrela – Sissingué – Tengrela;
2. L'axe routier Sud: Tengrela – Kanakono – Tengrela;
3. Le secteur Nord de la zone d'étude du permis comprenant Sissingué et environs;
4. Le secteur Sud de la zone d'étude du permis circonscrivant Kanakono sous préfecture et environs.

Dans ces secteurs au total 28 sites archéologiques ont été repérés. Leur analyse tient compte de leur nature et de leurs attributs fondés sur les caractéristiques morpho-techniques et typologiques des vestiges identifiés.

Les sites paléolithiques

Les sites paléolithiques sont équitablement répartis sur le permis: sur 10 cas attestés, cinq sont observables aussi bien dans la zone d'étude que dans les bandes des 500 mètres sur les axes routiers. Les vestiges relevant de cette époque n'ont été nulle part prélevés en association avec des témoins archéologiques, fussent-ils du néolithique ou du mésolithique. Cependant, le paléolithique est très faiblement représenté dans les bandes de 500 mètres, où il ne se manifeste plus que par l'existence des témoins des complexes culturels du Middle Stone Age (MSA) et du Sangoen. Sur l'axe Nord, deux points de prélèvement sont observables pour chaque complexe (Tialaka et Mbasso), tandis que sur l'axe Sud, l'on n'observe seulement qu'un seul point pour le MSA. En outre, les séries récoltées sont numériquement insignifiantes; mais elles montrent quelques formes déterminantes (nucléi discoïdes 2 pièces; pointes de type limaçoïde 1 pièce ou encore de type lupembien pour le MSA ; puis des bifaces à dos 2 pièces pour le Sangoen). Sur l'axe Sud, un point seulement de prélèvement (près de Pourou) pour le MSA est signalé et a livré un bien maigre inventaire.

La zone d'étude du projet s'étendant de Sissingué (au Nord) à Kanakono (au Sud) demeure selon les premiers indices, la zone de prédilection du peuplement paléolithique, surtout à Kakpolô grouillant d'orpailleurs clandestins venus du Mali et du Burkina Faso (figure 5).

FIGURE 5. KAKPOLO, ZONE DES ORPAILLEURS CLANDESTINS (PRES DE KANAKONO SOUS PREFECTURE)

En effet, l'inventaire des industries paléolithiques a révélé l'existence ici, de spécimens caractérisant toutes les étapes de l'évolution humaine dans cette région frontalière de la Côte d'Ivoire. Il s'agit des bifaces, des hachereaux, des bifaces à dos, des pics (Lioubine, Guédé 1999), des nucléi discoïdes, des pointes de type lupembien, des nucléi proto – et prismatiques) (figure 6).

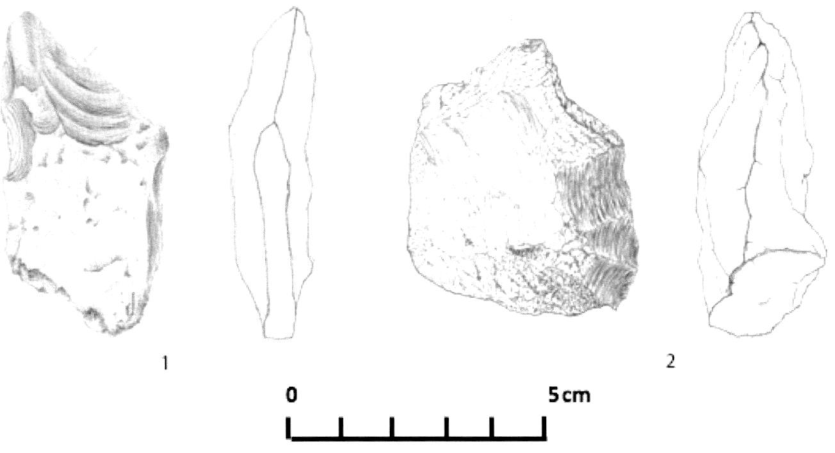

Figure 6. Exemple de becs de Tengrela

Ainsi, à l'exception de l'étape oldowaïenne qui n'est pas représentée, on distingue toutes les autres étapes allant du pléistocène moyen à supérieur (l'acheuléen moyen et supérieur, le Sangoen, le MSA et le paléolithique tardif). Tout cela est observable à Kakpolô, dans les dépôts constitués de roches polygéniques extraits et rejetés, pêle-mêle des puits par les orpailleurs clandestins. Une relecture de la colonne de ces dépôts appuyée par une fouille sondage (3 m x 3 m) devrait être, à souhait, programmée d'urgence pour rétablir ces industries lithiques dans leurs contextes stratigraphiques (figure 7).

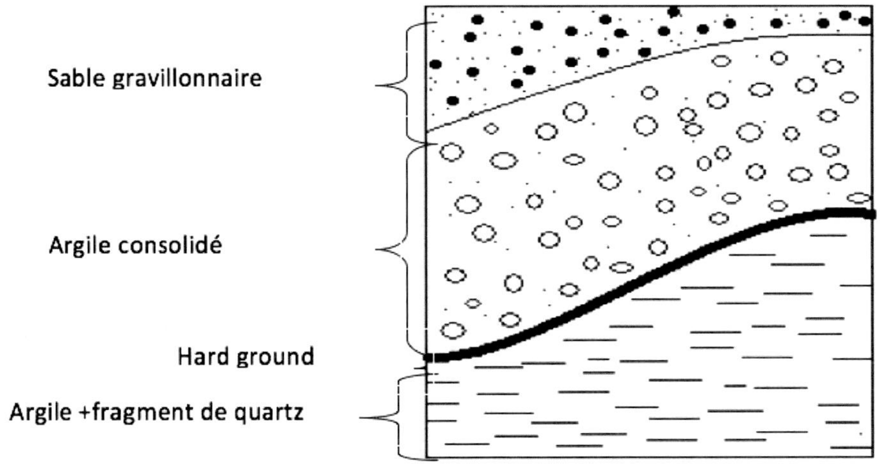

Figure 7. Formations observees a Kakpolo

Les sites néolithiques

Les témoins de l'époque néolithique constituent un bien maigre inventaire (01 pièce sur 04) comprenant une forme reconnue fossile directeur (hache taillée de 9 cm x 7 cm x 2,40 cm), prélevée en association avec des fragments de céramique, dans les sillons des labours d'une plaine cultivée (zone d'étude du projet à 2000 mètres au Nord-ouest de Kanakono). A côté de la hache, on distingue aussi une autre forme de belle facture: ciseau à double extrémité tranchante (10 cm x 4 cm x 2 cm), confectionné dans du quartz (figure 8).

Les gisements à fragments de céramique sont fortement présents dans la bande des 500 mètres sur les axes routiers Nord (Tengrela – Sissengué – Tengrela) et Sud (Tengrela – Kanakono – Tengrela).

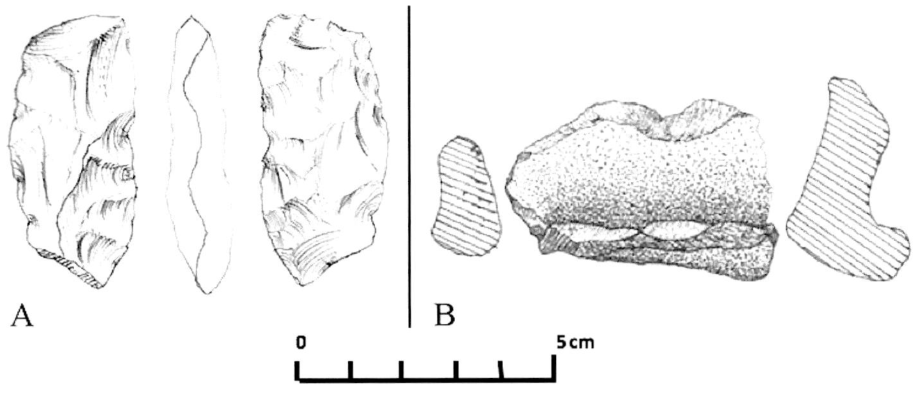

Figure 8. Outil lithique et ceramique; A: ciseau; B: fragment de ceramique (a paroi epaisse) associe aux vestiges lithiques)

Figue 9. Concentration de tessons ceramiques. Mbasso – Tialaka (axe routier Nord)

11 dont 6 localisés sur l'axe routier Nord (Tialaka – Mbasso; Sissengué – Mbasso) et cinq autres (05) sur l'axe Sud (Kanakono – Pourou; Pourou – Danzourou). Par rapport à la zone d'étude du projet, ces gisements sont faiblement représentés (3 cas, seulement, ont été observés au Nord-est et au Sud-ouest de Sissingué). La particularité de ce type de gisements réside dans le fait que les tessons de céramique exhumés par la charrue, lors des labours et collectés par les chercheurs pendant les investigations sont en réalité sans lien direct avec les vestiges lithiques. Dans certains cas, on les découvre en association avec les fragments des tuyères dans les sites de réduction (cas de Mbengué). Cela permet de supposer que ces gisements sont d'un âge plus récent que ceux où la céramique est associée aux vestiges lithiques.

Les sites métallurgiques

Les sites métallurgiques observés sur le terrain, au cours des recherches, sont situés dans la zone d'étude du projet, notamment au Sud-est de Sissingué. Ils se répartissent en deux catégories et peuvent s'identifier aux zones d'extraction et de réductions du minerai de fer.

Les zones d'extraction du minerai de fer

On distingue trois zones d'extraction du minerai de fer localisées dans le voisinage du rivage de la Bagoé soit environ 500 à 600 mètres de trajet. La première de ces mines de la métallurgie ancienne du fer est observable à 3400 mètres de Sissingué, sur la colline de 338 mètres d'altitude, dominant la vallée de la Bagoé. Cette colline est constituée de formations latéritiques dont plusieurs niveaux sont démantelés. Son plateau est tapissé d'une trentaine de trous circulaires creusés verticalement en profondeur (3 à 4 m) dans la cuirasse latéritique et qui se rejoignent dans une galerie souterraine. Leur diamètre varie de 80 à 120 cm. Ce site d'extraction du minerai de fer est le plus grand des trois mis au jour.

Le second site est situé à 450 m au Nord-est du précédent. Il présente des caractéristiques similaires au premier avec une vingtaine de trous de diamètre variant de 60 à 100 m. Le troisième et dernier site du genre est distant du second d'environ 1 km au Nord-est du précédent et est localisé sur une colline moins élevée que les deux premières. Il se caractérise également par la présence d'une fosse centrale, autour de laquelle gravitent 14 trous circulaires.

Les sites de réductions

Les sites de réductions représentent la deuxième catégorie de sites métallurgiques. Deux sur trois points sont totalement en ruines. Les seuls indices de leur existence se réduisent à la présence des fragments de tuyères et de vastes épandages de scories de fer (figure 10).

FIGURE 10A ET 10B. FOURNEAU ET FRAGMENT DE TUYERE DE TENGRELA;
10A © GUÉDÉ YIODÉ; 10B: © KOUASSI KOUAKOU SIMÉON

L'activité de la fonte du minerai de fer y avait sans doute prospéré. Ces deux points sont localisés au Nord-est de Sissingué, sur le flanc Est de la colline dominant le cours de la Bagoé. Ils sont distants l'un de l'autre de 200 mètres. Il pourrait s'agir en effet, d'un centre commun de métallurgistes. Le troisième point un peu plus au Nord, par rapport aux deux derniers, en est distant de 500 mètres.

Les dépôts de scories de fer couvrent dans cet espace une aire d'environ 150 m x 50 m, une altitude pouvant atteindre 1,50 à 2 mètres de haut et un diamètre de 3 mètres attestant une relative intensité de la fonte du fer. Des fragments de tuyères et de scories de fer ont été prélevés de même que quelques fragments de céramique associés à ces déchets. La position des fourneaux à proximité des zones d'extraction du minerai de fer suscite des questions. Celles-ci sont restées sans réponse à cause des délais de recherches trop courts. Ces questions demeurent une préoccupation majeure qui justifierait des recherches additionnelles permettant d'avoir une lisibilité relativement à: l'évaluation de l'importance des sites identifiés, la contribution à obtenir avec Occidental Gold S.A.R.L. Côte d'Ivoire sur les mesures de gestion des ressources archéologiques en vue de la mise en œuvre du projet. Ici également les résultats obtenus constituent une base pour l'orientation des recherches plus approfondies. Il s'agit:

1. De cartographier le secteur concerné;
2. De mettre en évidence une coupe des dépôts, d'où ont été extraits pêle-mêle les
3. Artéfacts repérés à partir de sondages ou fouilles.

L'importance des résultats obtenus à Hiré reflète la spécificité des recherches archéologiques en zone forestière. Celle-ci, dominée par un couvert végétal dense et une acidité prononcée du sol, détériore trop souvent les vestiges et empêche de voir, à leur juste valeur, l'importance de ces sites.

L'étape de Hiré

Les résultats obtenus sur le permis de Hiré selon les coordonnées (repères, sur la carte) appuyées par GPS peuvent être résumés sommairement comme suit: 17 sites découverts, dont 2 attribués au néolithique ; soit 15 sites paléolithiques observables aussi bien à l'Est d'Hiré (secteurs des aires d'exploitation et de stockage) qu'au Nord-ouest d'Hiré (zone d'aboutissement du minerai) pour 111 vestiges.

Trois points, seulement, de prélèvement ont été soumis à sondage pour récupérer méthodiquement les vestiges (Champ Emile et Mathias, N.-ouest d'Hiré). Les spécimens récoltés sont très variés (nucléi à enlèvements en désordre, à éclats, discoïdes, prismatiques) et représentatifs des complexes industriels connus en Côte d'Ivoire (Cf. Figure 10). Il ressort ainsi:

- Paléolithique tardif (2 sites dont 1 à l'Est d'Hiré et 1 au Nord-ouest);
- Middle Stone Age (MSA) (8 sites, dont 4 de part et d'autre);
- Sangoen (5 sites, dont 2 à l'Est d'Hiré et 3 au Nord-ouest).

Aucun vestige n'a représenté l'acheuléen. Deux sites néolithiques ont livré 17 vestiges dont 1 picoïde, 1 hache taillée, 1 meule dormante le tout associé de la céramique. Aucun site de la métallurgie ancienne du fer n'a été repéré.

Conclusion

Les investigations effectuées sur l'ensemble des zones susmentionnées ont permis de clarifier les environnements géomorphologiques des témoins archéologiques. Il s'agit d'une part, de dépôts de latérite démantelée sur les flancs des collines et d'autre part, des zones d'accumulation au bas des collines. Les vestiges archéologiques, caractérisant l'activité humaine, relèvent du pléistocène moyen à supérieur et le post-quaternaire. Une chronologie relative fondée sur les caractéristiques morpho-techniques et typologiques des outillages lithiques attestent ici, la représentation des étapes culturelles tels que les complexes acheuléens, sangoens, Middle Stone Age, paléolithique final, le néolithique et la métallurgie ancienne du fer (pour le post-quaternaire) dont la pratique sur toutes les aires culturelles en Côte d'Ivoire n'est plus à mettre en doute (Guédé 2003). Ces investigations qui ont révélé une diversité culturelle à l'époque préhistorique dans ces régions, contribuent de façon significative à l'enrichissement de la collection archéologique nationale, mais orientent aussi vers les problèmes prioritaires de leur valorisation et la protection des sites archéologiques. On peut saluer ici l'attention particulière que les entreprises Rangold, Occidental Gold et LGL attachent à l'existence et à l'importance des faits culturels en général et en particulier, du patrimoine archéologique du pays et de la protection de celui-ci. De ce point de vue, elles contribuent avec sérieux au développement de la recherche archéologique dans le territoire en ouvrant une nouvelle ère basée sur la promotion de l'archéologie préventive. Toute cette démarche initiée sous l'égide de ces sociétés d'extraction minière doit conduire à une prise de conscience généralisée. Elle devra permettre d'insister sur la nécessité de la mise en place d'une législation claire et appropriée qui conduise à des diagnostics en bonne et due forme, à des prescriptions et fouilles éventuelles en vue de la sauvegarde et la protection du patrimoine enfoui pour les générations futures. Aucun développement durable, est-il encore besoin de le rappeler, ne peut se concevoir davantage sans racines.

Références

Banque Mondiale (2005) – Politiques opérationnelles. PO 4.10. 13p.

Banque Mondiale (n.d.) Principes de sauvegarde du patrimoine culturel physique. Guide pratique. 163p.

Demoule, J. P.; Giligny, F.; Lehöerff, A. (2002) – Guide des méthodes de l'archéologie. La Découverte. Paris.

Guede, Y. (2003) – L'Afrique de l'Ouest, berceau de la métallurgie ancienne du fer (pour le compte du Patrimoine Culturel de Côte d'Ivoire) en collaboration avec le Musée Royal de l'Afrique Centrale et avec l'aide de la Coopération Belge au Développement. Salle des sciences. Tervuren. Catalogue.

Guede, Y. (2002) – Recherches paléolithiques dans le Haut Sassandra (Avril 1984-Août 1985): résultats préliminaires. Revue d'Histoire d'Art et d'Archéologie. Godo, 14: 7-27.

Lioubine, V. P.; Guede, Y. (1999) – Isslédovania paleolita V Zapadnoï Afriki (Respublika Kot d'Ivoir). Archéologuisheskii. Sankt-Peterbourg. Rossiiskaïa Akademia Nauk, 6: 19-40.

Philipe, J. (1998) – L'Archéologie. Belin. Paris.

Société Financière Internationale. (Octobre 1998) Politiques opérationnelles. OP 4.01. 14p.

CULTURAL RESOURCES, MANAGEMENT, PUBLIC POLICY, PEOPLE'S AWARENESS AND SUSTAINABLE DEVELOPMENT

SESSION 15 C

Edited by

Ranjana Ray and Vidula Jayswal

A study of the Archaeological sites of the Birbhum District, Bengal – Its management and sustainable development

Asmita Basu
Lecturer, Academy for Professional Excellence (APEX), Guest Faculty,
Goenka College of Commerce & B.A., Kolkata, India
asmita.basu2011@gmail.com

Abstract

Culturally rich and studded with a number of temples and heritage sites, Birbhum, a significant temple town in Eastern India, has been an important area of study. In the present scenario, sustainable development has become an important challenge to deal with particularly in the age of modernization. Correlation and cooperation needs to be established between archaeology and the new age principles of management. The present study aims to highlight the growing challenges and possible remedies of sustainable development of archaeological sites through a case study of the temple sites in the Birbhum district. The materials have been collected through the field work in this region. Some important temple sites have been selected for the purpose of the study namely- the Temple sites of Supur, Ghurisha and Jaydev –kenduli on the bank of the Ajay river.

Key words

Archaeological sites, terracotta temples, cultural heritage, sustainability

Resume

Culturellement riche et parsemée d'un grand nombre de temples et de sites patrimoniaux, Birbhum, une importante ville temple de l'Inde orientale, a été un champ d'étude significatif. Dans le scénario actuel, le développement durable est devenu un défi important à relever en particulier dans l'ère de la modernisation. La corrélation et la coopération doivent être établies entre l'archéologie et les nouveaux principes de gestion. La présente étude vise à mettre en évidence les défis croissants et les recours possibles du développement durable des sites archéologiques à travers une étude de cas des sites de temple dans le district de Birbhum. Les matériaux ont été recueillis à travers le travail de terrain dans cette région. Certains sites importants de temple ont été sélectionnés pour cette étude, à savoir les sites du temple de Supur, Ghurisha et Jaydev-kenduli sur la rive de la rivière Ajay.

Mots-clés

Sites archéologiques, temples en terre cuite, patrimoine culturel, durabilité

Introduction

Extraordinarily rich, vast and diverse cultural heritage in the form of built heritage, archaeological sites and remains since the ancient times are the symbols of both cultural expression and evolution. Ancient temples have been considered as the major sources of various religious faiths, philosophical aspects, cultural and architectural heritages. Birbhum, the land of the red soil' is also referred to as 'the land of the brave' in the state of West Bengal in eastern India.

Geographically the district of Birbhum is positioned between 23°33' and 24°35' north latitude and between 87°10' and 88°2' east longitude. It stretches over an area of 1752 square miles. The district shares its boundaries with two other districts of West Bengal itself viz. Murshidabad and Burdwanand the Santhal Pargana of the neighbouring state of Jharkhand as well (figure 1). It is a triangular tract of land being bordered on the north and west by Santhal Pargana (Jharkhand) and the district of Murshidabad, on the east by the districts of Murshidabad and Burdwan. The southern part of Birbum district shares its boundary with the district of Burdwan, being only separated by the river Ajay (O'Malley 1910:1). The district is endowed with a number of rivers and rivulets running from west to east having marginal inclination towards south. The rivers Ajay, Mayurakshi and Kopai

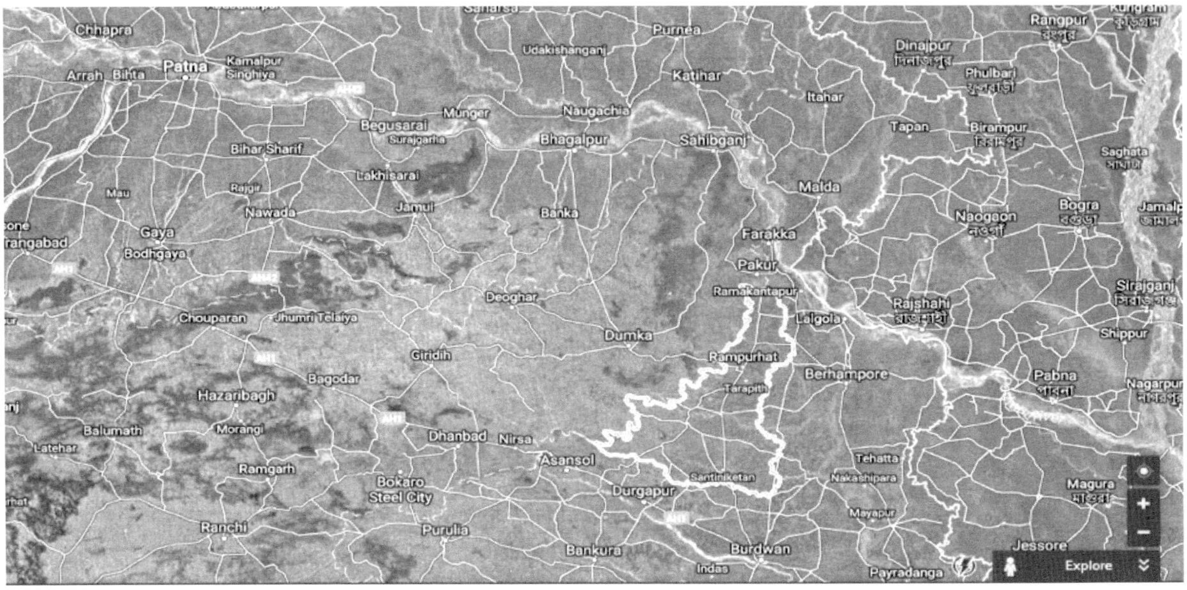

FIGURE 1. SATELLITE IMAGERY OF BIRBHUM DISTRICT

are significant rivers of this region. Of these rivers, Ajay and Mayurakshi also known as Mor, have considerable size and while the former constitutes the southern boundary of Birbhum, the latter flows across the district from West to East. Birbhum was a constituent part of ancient Rarh region of Bengal particularly the northern part of Rarh.

The name Birbhum might have originated from the Mundari word 'Bir' meaning 'forest.' It is indeed a land of heritages bearing the rich history of different cultures and sects. There are a number of archaeological sites in this region. Excavations have been undertaken at different periods of time. A few of the important sites of this region can be located at Nanur, Ghurisha, Supur, Surul, Kenduli, Itanda etc. Some of these sites are protected by ASI and state Government while some are private temples, unprotected till date.

Birbhum is a significant temple town in Eastern India dominated by several brave kings since the early time. Remnants of various human cultures from pre-historic to late medieval period add profound archaeological and historical importance to the region. Culturally rich and studded with a number of temples and heritage sites, Birbhum has been an important area of study. Temples of this region combine harmony and symmetry with a high quality of outer embellishments. There are numerous terracotta temples belonging to the late medieval period. Ajay being a river of great magnitude, its banks have housed human settlements through various eras and has also been a notable site for temple construction. For the purpose of the present study some of the important temple sites have been selected namely– the Temple sites of Supur, Ghurisha and Jaydev –kenduli on the bank of the Ajay river (figure 2a and 2b).

The village of Supur is located on the eastern part of Birbhum district, 5km south of the small but famous town of Shantiniketan, the abode of the great poet Rabindrath Tagore. In this small village we come across the twin terracotta Shiva temple (figure 3) which dates back to 1717 A.D. The temples have been built on a raised platform next to each other. One of these is octagonal in shape with curved tower and is beautifully decorated with terracotta figures on each of its eight walls. The terracotta figures on the walls are usually that of Hindu deities with illustrations of various mythologies and legends. The other temple has a square base and similar type of curved tower. The walls of this square shaped temple are also embellished with terracotta figures. A narrow wooden door with intricate

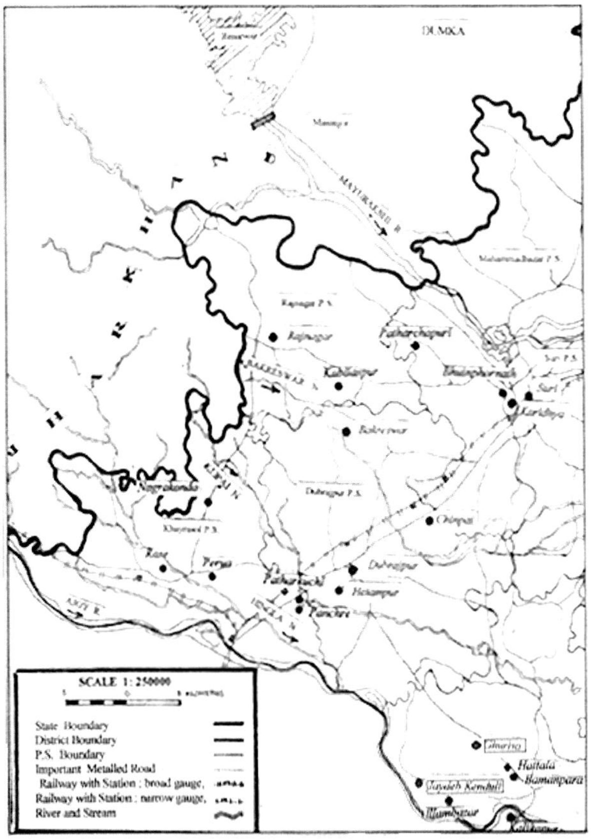

Figure 2a. Map showing temple sites in the western part of Birbhum (© P. Mukherjee)

Figure 2b. Map showing temple sites in the eastern part of Birbhum (© P. Mukherjee)

carvings leads the entrance of each of the temples. This temple site is under the purview of the Department of Archaeology, Government of West Bengal (Mukherjee 2010, 61).

Temple site of Supur

The village of Supur is located on the eastern part of Birbhum district, 5 km south of the small but famous town of Shantiniketan, the abode of the great poet Rabindrath Tagore. In this small village we come across the twin terracotta Shiva temple (figure 3) which dates back to 1717 A.D. The temples have been built on a raised platform next to each other. One of these is octagonal in shape with curved tower and is beautifully decorated with terracotta figures on each of its eight walls. The terracotta figures on the walls are usually that of Hindu deities with illustrations of various mythologies and legends. The other temple has a square base and similar type of curved tower. The walls of this square shaped temple are also embellished with terracotta figures. A narrow wooden door with intricate carvings leads the entrance of each of the temples. This temple site is under the purview of the Department of Archaeology, Government of West Bengal (Mukherjee 2010, 61).

Temple site of Ghurisha

Ghurisha is a small village in the district of Birbhum lying on the western side. It is situated at a distance of 30 km from the town of Shantiniketan. In this village, a mound with a Muslim burial place on top of it has been reported and ruins of lateritic temple have been found from this area but the details of the mound and the temple ruins has not been formally published (Chakraborty 2001:110). Remarkably in this village we find a beautifully adorned terracotta temple. This temple

FIGURE 3. SIVA TEMPLE IN SUPUR

is unprotected and privately maintained. The temple is locally known as the Gopal Mandir which is a ratna temple (figure 4). It has nine ratnas or shikharas, a popular style of temple architecture in Bengal. The temple is a brick temple built on a high platform dated 1768 A.D. The exterior walls have impressive terracotta embellishments. Terracotta panels with images of various Hindu gods and goddesses, Krishna-lila panels are worth mentioning (Mukherjee 2010, 122-123).

FIGURE 4. GOPAL MANDIR (TEMPLE) IN GHURISHA.

Temple site of Jaydev-Kenduli

Jaydev-Kenduli is a village on the bank of Ajay river, on the western side of Birbhum. It is 35 km south-west of Shantiniketan. The village of Jaydev-Kenduli holds great significance as the birth place of the eminent court poet of the King Lakshmanasena belonging to Sena dynasty of Bengal during 12th century A.D. The region is rich in archaeological remains (Chakraborty 2001, 107). An exquisite Navaratna temple known as Radha-Vinod temple is housed in this village (figure 5). It is a protected site by Archaeological Survey of India. It has nine shikharas and stands on a raised platform. The extensively carved terracotta panels (figure 6) portray scenes from Ramayana, Mahabharata, Krishna-lila and other mythological stories (Mukherjee 2010:141).

Figure 5. Radha-Vinod temple in Jaydev-Kenduli

Figure 6. Terracotta Panel From Radha-Vinod Temple In Jaydev-Kenduli

Management and sustainable development

The rich cultural heritage usually reflects the diverse historical background and origins of people which leads to the development of the present day human culture and civilization of a particular region. Since the cultural heritage of a nation or a specific region is unique and irreplaceable so it is important to properly manage these heritages. It should be noted that them is management of cultural resources can lead to irreversible damage and loss of essential information about a culture's past. To sustain the cultural heritages for the future generations, an integrated and holistic management approach is inevitable. A mere process of preservation and conservation of the heritage sites cannot provide sustainability to the built heritages. It is immensely vital to balance the contemporary needs of the local community and the wider society, connected to the recent global concepts with the help of modern management principles and the archaeological resources. At the onset of this management process we need to identify the attributes which are common to the diverse range of cultural objects and heritages. These features are essential for the decision-making process and should be considered while evaluating the importance of cultural heritage, its management, conservation and protection, ensuring the sustainability of such cultural legacy. These vital attributes which are similar in all cultural heritages are as follows:

1. Uniqueness: Every cultural resource, be it historic monuments, buildings, archaeological sites or living shrines, can be distinctly identified by the virtue of its historic character, aesthetics and inherent worth. Although uniqueness of a heritage site or object does not imply higher value, it is a vital feature which should be considered in the decision-making process.
2. Irreplaceable: Tangible cultural heritage is a limited or non-renewable resource. This type of heritage cannot be replaced or reproduced if it is damaged or lost. Such a loss of cultural heritage may imply the loss of vital information related to a country or a loss for a scope of socio-economic development of a nation. It can also lead to the problem of linking a particular culture to its historic background and tradition.
3. Value to communities: In order to evaluate the actual worth of a nation's cultural heritage, it is important to realize its significance to one or more communities. In order to be significant a particular cultural resource needs to be linked with the cultural context and should have historic, scientific, technological connections with the specific community and the nation as a whole.

Thus, before proceeding with the management of archaeological sites, we need to assess all the essential factors and then formulate a proper plan with the help of suitable management principles particularly proper strategies should be implemented.

Need for sustainability of Temple sites

The area under the purview of this study is historically rich consisting of a wide a variety of built structures like terracotta temples. It is this cultural treasure which unfolds the challenge of sustainability for the present generation. It is of immense concern how to protect and preserve these national assets for the future generations.

To sustain the heritage sites, we need to combine the principles of two disciplines namely- archaeology and management. At the very initial stage the basic principle of strategic planning put forward by the discipline of strategic management should be applied. Strategic planning can be referred to as long range planning. It generally involves the development of mission, objectives, strategies and policies of a corporation. (Wheelen *et al.* 2006, 100). A very widely used tool by organisations for analysing the internal and external factors is SWOT or TOWS analysis which represents Strength, Weakness, Opportunities and Threats and TOWS just the opposite of it. SWOT analysis has a number of benefits. This tool of strategic planning is very simple to use, low cost, addresses and clarifies various issues. It serves as a starting point for strategic analysis. It also generates various goal-oriented alternatives and more importantly it can be modified as per the changing scenario (Kazmi 2011, 71-72).

For the management of archaeological sites similar type of strategic planning must be conducted at the very onset. Considering the three temples sites of Birbhum, chosen for the present study, have been analysed under the light of management principles and the strategic plan has been evolved. The SWOT matrix has been prepared for the temple sites in Birbhum.

By analysing the figure 7, we can get an idea about the strengths and weaknesses of this region particularly of the temple sites chosen for this study. This analysis is conducted at the preliminary stage which helps to develop the strategic plan and competitive advantages for the archaeological sites. Furthermore, the information obtained on the opportunities that are available, will help us to take adequate measures and construct a sustainable framework. This framework is not only meant for the sustainability of the temples but also the surrounding region and more importantly the people residing in that region. Since these villages are remotely located the transportation and communication networks are not well developed. People specially the tourists are hardly aware of such archaeological gems located in these villages. So there is a great scope for developing cultural tourism in this region. Site museums can be constructed which will attract tourists and also generate awareness among the local people. A proper model has to be planned and implemented in which the local people will form the base. They will get the benefits such as employment, socio-economic development, market for local craftsmanship etc.

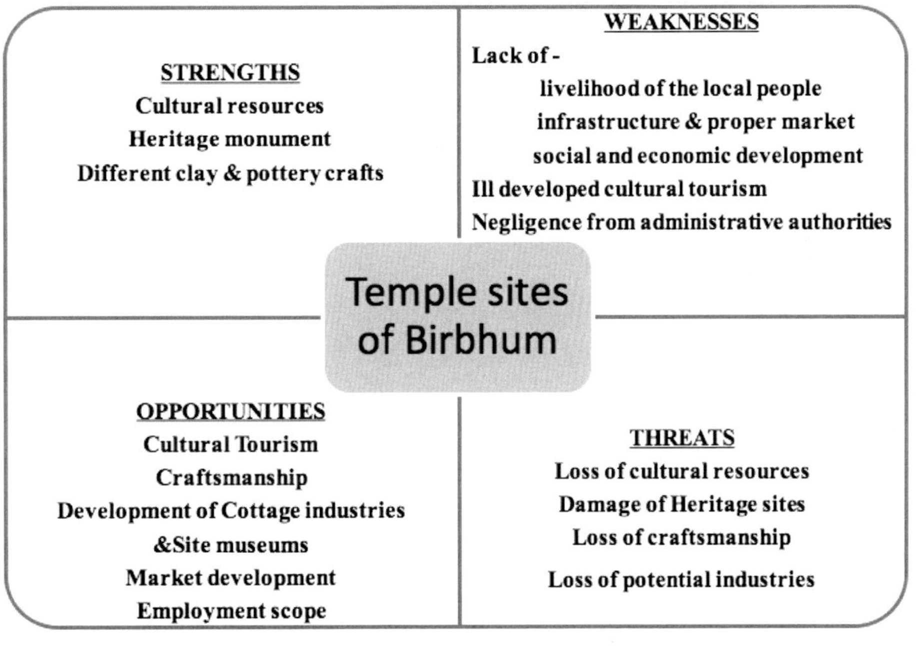

Figure 7. SWOT matrix for the archaeological sites of temple sites of Birbhu

Conclusion

The study reveals that Birbhum has ample number of archaeological sites and cultural heritages which can be used as a base for sustainable development of the region. It should be noted that the process of sustainable development needs a multi-disciplinary approach and cannot achieve its goal by a solitary endeavour. Government departments and agencies alone cannot protect all these heritage monuments as they are huge in number. In the disciple of management studies, we come across the concept of Corporate Social Responsibility (CSR). Traditionally, CSR refers to businesses' responsibility to act ethically and consider their impacts on the community as a whole. As per CSR norms the companies need to do something for the development of the society. At present, in India, companies are funding different projects vital for social development in order to meet the CSR norms. So if the neglected heritage sites can be highlighted, then the corporate funding can be brought in those areas which can help to generate the required structure for sustainable development.

Thus, in conclusion we may say that the cohesion between the two disciplines namely- archaeology and strategic management will not only lead to the sustainable development of the archaeological sites but also to the economic growth and development of the region. Unprotected monuments and heritages in danger can be revived with the help of building a bridge with the Corporate as well as other Government and Non- Government agencies. Financial support and infrastructure development could be the key support obtained from the corporate world for the sustainability of the sites.

References

Chakraborty, D. (2001) – *Archaeological Geography of the Ganga Plain- The Lower and Middle Ganga.* Delhi: Permanent Black.

Kazmi, A. (2011) – *Strategic Management and Business Policy.* New Delhi: Tata McGraw Hill Education Pvt. Ltd.

Mukherjee, P. (Eds.) (2010) – *Monuments around Shantiniketan.* Gurgaon: Shubhi Publications.

O'Malley, L. S. S. (1910) – *Bengal District Gazetteers-Birbhum.* Calcutta: The Secretariat Book Depot.

Wheelen, T. L.; Hunger, J. D.; Rangarajan, K. (2006) – *Concepts in Strategic Management and Business Policy.* Delhi: Pearson Education.

A Study of Prehistoric Cultural Heritage and Management in Odisha, India

Debasis Kumar Mondal
Assistant Professor, Department of Anthropology, University of Calcutta
anth.debasis@gmail.com

Abstract

Heritage management is a current issue of the twenty first century over the world. In most of the cases emphasis is given on historical sites and monuments rather than prehistoric sites. Present study is an approach to know the status of prehistoric sites of Odisha, one of the major states of eastern part of India. A number of sites have been explored and reported from different parts of the state. For present study two sites of northern part of Odisha were selected for in depth research about the natural and human agencies responsible for the destruction of the sites and cultural remains and finally the exploration of the remedial measures for the protection and/or preservation of those prehistoric sites were made.

Key words

Heritage, Management, Prehistory, Site Destruction, Natural Causes, Human Activity, Awareness, Policies

Introduction

The concept of heritage is changing day by day with its enormous expansion and broadening of definitions. The identification of cultural heritage and its management is increasing significantly all over the world. In broadest sense heritage primarily includes urban centers, archeological sites, industrial heritage, cultural land scape and heritage routes. The present focus is on the archeological sites and specifically the identification and preservation of prehistoric sites in Indian context. The concept of preservation of heritage in India started in 1873. In this year Central Government issued a circular assigned to local Government regarding the preservation and caring of monuments which have historical and architectural value during the time of Cunnigman (Roy, 2011). With the UNESCO declaration, Cultural Heritage Management (CHM) became an urgent issue globally since 1972. So, the concept of heritage management was developed very early with the initial phase of archeology in India. The present study is an endeavor to study the status of management of prehistoric cultural heritage of India with special emphasis on Odisha. Odisha (formerly known as Orissa) is a state of India famous as a pilgrimage Centre and tourist spots. It lies on the eastern coast of the Indian subcontinent. The root of the cultural heritage of Odisha goes back to its prehistoric origin. Since 1939 a number of prehistoric surveys have been carried out in the different districts of Odisha. There are number of reported sites starting from Paleolithic to Neo-Chalcolithic period distributed in almost all over the states in different geographical settings. Most of the sites are open air sites and located at the river bank. So the erosional activity of the River is destroying the site day by day and dislocating the artifacts from its stratified zone. A number of attempts have been made both from State Government and central Government to protect different historical monuments. The prehistoric sites remained in dark and damages resulted both from natural and human activities, such as agriculture, looting, hunting and industrial activities. Present paper is an in-depth study to identify the problems and remedial measures for protecting the rich prehistoric heritage of Odisha, India.

Objectives

There is an attempt to study the management of prehistoric cultural resources of Odisha, India. The study also highlights the major threats against the protection of these prehistoric sites and suggestive remedies to preserve this site which may unfold the history of ethnic migration, diffusion of culture, trade, religion, different crafts, people and other aspects of the society.

Methodology

For the present study two sites Shigarh in Angul district and Kuanr in Keonjhar district of Odisha have been selected. Different field methods involving exploration, both extensive and intensive survey have been carried out to know the distribution and extension of the sites, geographical and geological location to understand the nature of the sites. Different agencies responsible for destruction of the sites, such as deforestation, soil erosion, and displacement of the layer and riverine activities also have been observed. Observation is an important tool to identify the nature of the sites, distribution of artifacts and the process of destruction. Interviewing of local people also has been conducted to gather information about the history of the site, present activities and their opinion for protection of the site. The research papers, books and journals containing the information were done as far as possible as secondary sources.

Physiography of Odisha

The state Odisha lies in the eastern part of India between $17^{0}49'$ to $22^{0}34'$ N latitude and from $81^{0}23'$ to $87^{0}29'$ E longitude. Odisha is the tenth biggest state of India consisted of thirty districts with an area of 155,707 sq. km. 30.3% of the total geographical area of the state is covered by forest. The population is 31.659,736 according to 1991 census. Physiographically Odisha has been divided into five different geomorphological zones: the Coastal Plain in the east, the Middle Mountainous and Highlands Region, the Central plateaus, the western rolling uplands and the major flood plains. The northern part is an extension of Chotanagpur plateau and the middle mountainous highland region comprises of hills and mountains of the Eastern Ghats. These two major regions are separated by the river Mahanadi. The principal rivers of Odisha are Mahanadi, Brahmani, Baitarani, Burhabalang and Suvernarekha. Out of these rivers Mahanadi, Brahmani and Baitarani have formed a compound delta along the coast of Bay of Bengal and also formed a watershed. As the state is full of rivers, the

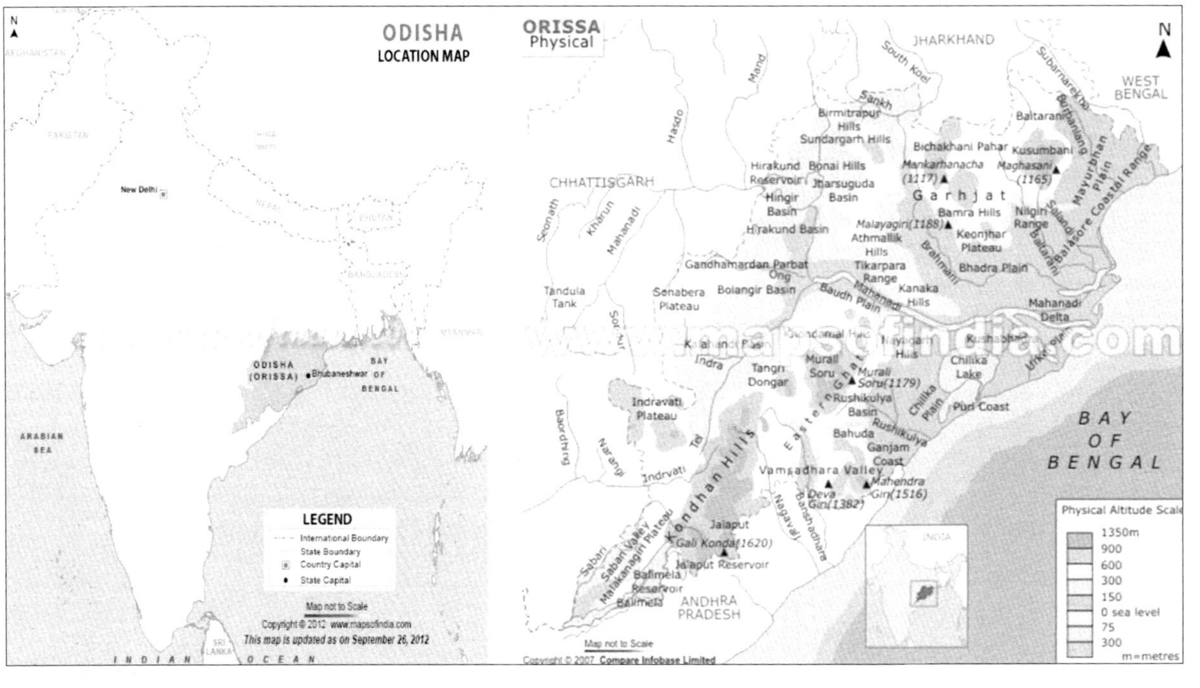

FIGURE 1. LOCALIZATION OF THE AREA (SOURCE: HTTP://WWW.MAPSOFINDIA.COM)

valleys are very fertile and thickly populated. As its location near the tropic of cancer the climate of Odisha is tropical monsoon type. There is widespread rainfall varies from 181 cm. to 101 cm. Forest vegetation is primarily tropical deciduous and thickly forest zones have preserved many wild animals. Geologically the land mass is very old in origin. The geological formations from Archean age to Pleistocene have been found from different parts of the state. Laterites, river gravels, older alluvium, raised beaches are the Pleistocene formation. Alluvium and wind-blown sand are recent in origin. Odisha has varieties of rocks of different geological ages like khandalite, granite, charnockite, and quartzite etc. Basalt is also common in such areas. Prehistoric man selected primarily quartzite and occasionally basalt for making tools. Chert and quartz from veins of the rocks were also used as raw materials during Middle and late Stone Age cultures. There are many tribal groups living in different geophysical settings. About sixty two tribal communities have been noted and they preserve indigenous cultural tradition sometimes have similarities with prehistoric culture (Bhatt 2008) (Figure 1).

Prehistoric cultural heritage of Odisha

A number of explorations and excavations have been conducted in different parts of the state starting systematically from 1939. Attempts have been made by Archaeologists, Anthropologists, Geologists and Prehistorians to know the cultural sequence, evolution and variation of different prehistoric cultural traits with the different parts of the world. A number of ethno-archeological studied also have been conducted to study the ethnographic parallels of prehistoric culture among the different indigenous populations distributed in different geophysical settings.

Paleolithic Culture

In 1875 V. Ball recorded Paleolithic artifacts from the districts of Angul (Kaliakata), Talcher (Harichandanpur), Sambalpur (Bursapali) and Dhenkanal (Ball 1876). After a long period of Ball's discovery P. Acharya and E. C. Worman discovered the famous Lower Paleolithic site Kuliana in Mayurbhanj district of Northern Odisha in 1939. Kuliana is the first excavated Paleolithic site of India by Nirmal Kumar Bose and Dharani Sen of the Department of Anthropology, University of Calcutta (Bose and Sen 1948). Other sites yielded Lower Paleolithic artifacts are Kamarpal, Kamta, Kalabaria, Koilisuta, Nuaberi, Pariakoli. These sites are distributed around the Burhabalang River. In 1948 stone tools were found from two lateritic gravel quarries at Bangiriposi on the left bank of the river Burhabalang by D. Sen and G. S. Ray. (Sen *et. al.* 1956). Mohapatra explored the districts of Dhenkanal, Sundergarh, Sambalpur, Keonjhar and Mayurbhanj from 1957 to 1959. The region mainly covered the northern part of Odisha and the sites are categorized according to the location along the different river valleys (Mohaptra 1962).

Sites in the Brahmani river valley and its tributaries: Kharagprasad, Talcher, Bhalitundi, Kulei, Bhimkand, Chakrasil, Harichandanpur, Kankili, Hindol Road, Samal, Jangra or Jangla, Bonaigarh, Bhaludungri, Tumkelaghat, Palalhara, Kaliakata, Parang, Kurhadi, Khuntagaon, Khadiakudur, Bhanjgarh, Bisra, Jagannathposh, Jhirpani, Satkuta, Bonaikala, Barmanda, Rairangpur, Bahalda, Badra, Bijatala, Bisai, Kandalia. Other sites in the Burhabalang river valley and its tributaries: Domukhani, Mahulia, Pratappur, Banspal, Jirda, Mendakhai, Ghantasila, Champua, Ramla, Jagannathpur, Patna, Udaipur, Barasol; in the Mahanadi River valley and its tributaries: Tikarpara, Bhasma, Bishalbury; in the Suvarnarekha River valley: Sisra.

A number of prehistoric sites were explored from Khiching area and Simlipal Massif in Mayurbhanj district (Chakrabarti 1990, 2000). Tripathy (1980) explored the South Odisha and discovered a number of Paleolithic sites. Kalma in the right bank of the River Bamshadhara, Kharligarh at the right bank of the river Raul which is a tributary of Tel River, Madabhati at the left bank of the River Raul, Ratakhandi at the confluence of the River Tel and Raul, Sandi Sara and Bhuanpada at the bank of the River Tel.

The Paleolithic culture of Mayurbhanj is also studied by number of scholars (D. K. Chakrabarti 1993, S. Chakrabarti 1990; Mohanty *et al.* 1997). A rich evidence of Lower Paleolithic culture has been found from the Brahmani Valley in Dhenkanal district in central Odisha (Sing 1985). The other reported sites are Kuchinda (Ratha and Bhattacharya 1988) and Burla (Behra *et al.* 1996; Sharma 1994; Basa and Mohanta 1999) in the middle Mahanadi Valley.

Upper Paleolithic sites are also reported from Indravati Basin (Nanda 1982-83), Burla in the middle Mahandi valley (Sharma 1994), upper Brahmani valley in Sundargarh district (Behera 1989) and Mayurbhanj (Mishra 1990).

Upper Paleolithic tools were recorded from 17 open air sites in the Koraput region. Recent exploration in middle Brahmani Valley yielded 15 lower Paleolithic sites (Swain and Bhoi 2010).

The lower Paleolithic culture of Odisha is also termed as Early Stone Age culture. The cultural assemblages show three stages of development. The stage I comprises of Hand axe, irregular flaked bifaces, flakes, scrapers characterised by Block-on-Block technique. The primary tool types of Stage II are Hand axes, Cleavers, Scrapers, Cores, Flakes and predominant technique was cylinder hammer technique. Stage III also comprises the tool types of stage II including both the large and miniature varieties. They became master over the cylinder hammer technique and secondary retouching and finishing. The tool types of Middle Paleolithic period (Middle Stone Age) are smaller flake tools like scraper, borer, burin, point. Different types of scrapers are Side scrapers, End scrapers, Hollow scrapers, Round scrapers. The upper Paleolithic culture was not distinguished in Odisha. But recent explorations yielded upper Paleolithic industry which is comprises of blade, burin, knife, denticulates, notches borer, burin, baked blades though it is difficult to put these culture in proper stratified zone.

Mesolithic Culture

Mesolithic culture of Odisha is very widespread in Northern, Central and South Central Odisha. 85 microlithic sites were reported from the Indrabati basin in South Odisha (Nanda 1982-83; 1984). Mesolithic assemblages also have been found from 30 open air sites in Phulbani from South-central Odisha (Ota 1986). Other concentration of microliths have been reported from Jira basin (Misra 1982-83), 1b valley (Tripathy 1982-83), Deo valley Khairi-Bandhan valley, Kharkai valley, (Mohanty *et. al.* 1997), Duburi-Tamaka and Darpan Khas area of Jaipur (Sahoo 1987). About 69 Mesolithic sites also have been reported from Keonjhar district by Mohanty (1989, 2000). Other noticeable Mesolithic sites are Khiching area (Chakraborty 1990) in Mayurbhanj district. In Sundargarh district microliths have been reported from Upper Mahanadi Valley (Behera 1989), Manikmunda (IAR 1991-92), Giripur (IAR 1991-92), Sukhamankar (IAR 1993-94), Hemangir-Kanika region (IAR 1992-93). Tripathy (2000) identified 14 Mesolithic sites in the Mahanadi and Sulunki Valley in Boudh district. Microliths of Odisha comprised of both non geometric and geometric microliths like lunate, triangle, trapeze with heavy duty tools like scrapers, chopper and pointed tools which were used for clearing of forest, carpentry, construction of houses and processing of food (Mohanty 1989). The subsistence pattern and economy has resembled of local indigenous communities.

Neolithic Culture

The first reported Neolithic site in Odisha was reported by Acharya (1923-24) from Baidyapur in Mayurbhanj district. Later discovery has been done by R. D. Banerji (1930) and E. C. Worman Jr. (1949). Kuchai is an excavated site near Budhabalanga River in Mayurbhanj district (Thapar 1985). Evidences of Neolithic culture have been reported from Budhabalanga, Kharkai, Deo river valley in Mayurbhanj district (Basa 1984), Brahmani Valley in Dhenkanal district, Mankada valley around Pallahara area in Angul district in Central Odisha (Basa *et. al.* 2000), Keonjhar (Mohanty 1992), Sundargarh (Majumder, 1955, Mahapatra 1962, Tripathy 1982-83, Behera 1989, 2000), Bolangir (Tripathy 1972), Phulbani (ota 1986), Sambalpur (Misra 1982-83), Cuttack (Lal 1953), Puri (IAR

1984-85: 59-60), Koraput (Pustry 1972) and Ganjam (I.A.R. 1956-57: 340-31), Mayurbhanj (Tripathy 1966). Neolithic site of Coastal Odisha is Golabai Period I (Sinha 2000). Other important sites of middle Mahanadi valley are Lahanda and Hirakud, Hikudi (Behera 2013), Sulabdih (Behera 1992). Mohanta (2001) has reported 39 Neolithic sites in Mayurbhanj and Keonjhar district of northern Odisha. 25 Neolithic sites also have been reported by D. Sahoo around the Lower Mahanadi valley between Cuttack and Jajpur districts. A review of Neolithic culture of Orissa has been done by Dash (2000), Sahoo and Basa (2013).

The Neolithic culture of Odisha has been found both in the plateaus, hilly areas and plain land of coastal Odisha. Neolithic people produce rice and pulses. The agricultural economy was also supported by animal husbandry and hunting gathering. Fishing was common in sites near coastal areas. The tool types are divided into two. One is celt component which comprises of axes, adzes, chisels, and shouldered axes; other types include ring-stone, ring ball, arrowhead, pestle, saddle quern and polishers. Beside these artifacts Odishan Neolithic has diversified tool types like heavy duty tools, microliths with different types of pot sherds primarily Red ware.

Chalco-Neolithic Culture

A number of Chalco-Neolithic sites have been discovered in Central Odisha i.e. Sankerjang in Dhenkanal district, Central Odisha (Yule *et. al.*1989, 2000), Golbai Sasan (Sinha 1990-91, 2000) in Khurda district, Gopalpur (Kar 1995-96, 2000) in Nayagarh district. Chalco-Neolithic culture of Northern Odisha was first reported from Kuanr (Ray 1993, Ray *et. al.* 2000) in Keonjhar district and Khambeswaripali in Suvarnapur district of Western Odisha (Behera 2006). Chalcolithic culture of Odisha was emerged during the 2nd millennium BCE. It is characterised by the use of copper and its alloys with stone tools. The stone tools are predominantly polished axes with heavy duty tools and microliths. The evidences of different types of crafts have been found such as pottery, terracotta, bead making, metallurgy, bone tool making etc. The subsistence level of this period is more or less same with the Neolithic period (Ray and Mondal 2013) and established an important phase in the origin and development of complex society in Odisha (Sahoo and Basa 2013).

Present undertakings

Two sites have been selected for the present study. One is the site Shigarh in Angul district of Odisha. The site is unique in the sense that there is a continuity of culture from lower Paleolithic to Neolithic period. Another is Kuanr in Keonjhar district of Odisha. This is a Chalco-Neolithic site yielded important aspects of indigenous metallurgy developed independently in the area. Different aspects of destruction of site have been observed through the field survey.

Site Shigarh in Angul district of Odisha

The site Shigarh ($21^{0}27'$ North, $85^{0}12'$ East) is a prehistoric site which located by the bank of the river Mankara, a tributary of Brahmani in Angul district of Northern Odisha. The site is extended between 160 m to 200 m contour line at the foothills of Mankarachua which is a reserve forest covered with tropical deciduous vegetation. The area is bounded by the Mankarchua reserve forest at the North, Tamkia reserve forest at the North East and Mankara River at the South flows from East-West direction. The site is on the table land undulating and rolling in nature. A number of outcrops primarily composed of quartz and quartzite covered the area. There is a hill stream locally known as Makarachua nallah originates from Mankarchua hill. It remains dry during summer and winter and full of water during rainy season. This is the sources of water to the local people of the area. Boulders and gravels are deposited along with the nullah. The soil is lateritic and sandy in nature. At the westward alluvium has been found, which is yellowish and sandy in nature. This part of the area is used for agricultural purpose. Tools are concentrated along the nullah and at the exposed stratigraphic sections.

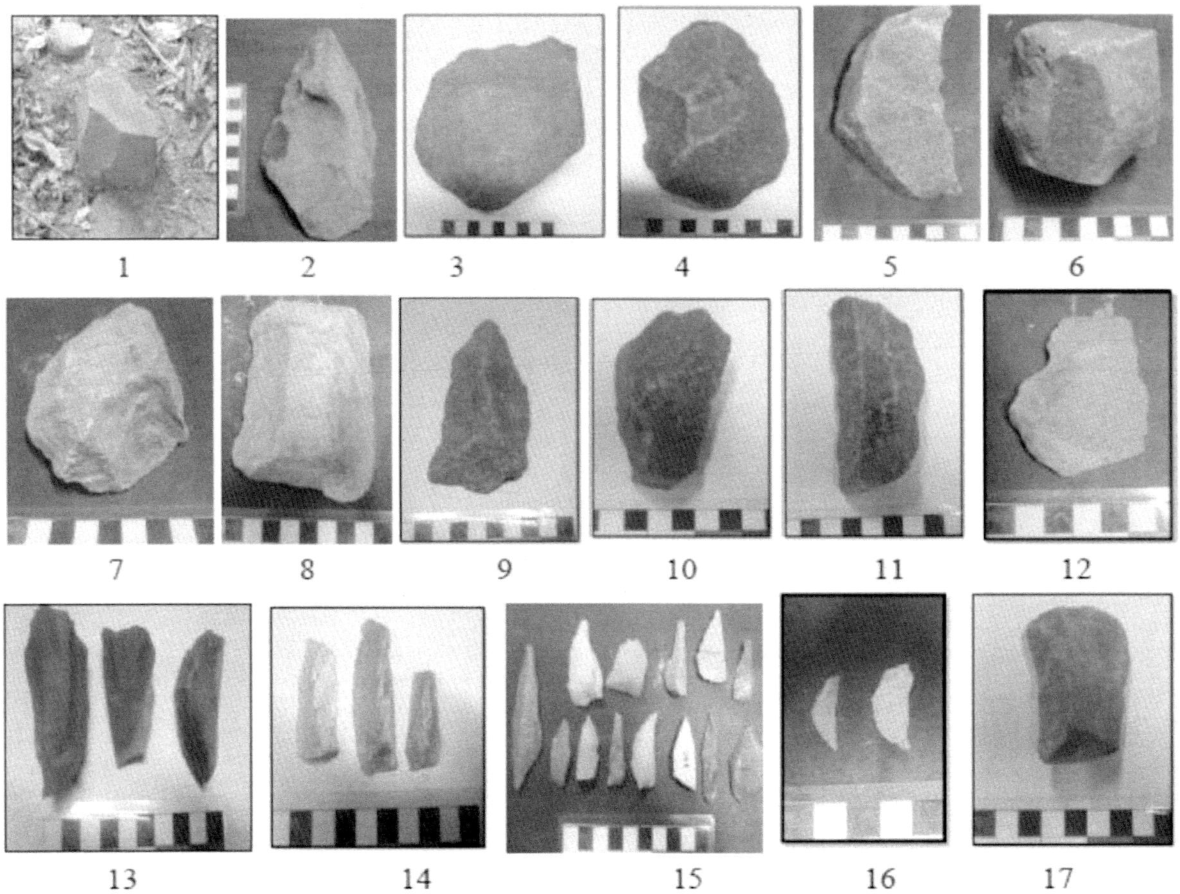

1. Anvil, 2. Hand axe, 3. Chopper, 4. Double sided scrapers, 5. Concave scrapers, 6. Core 7. Tortoise core, 8. Side Cum end scrapers, 9. Point, 10. End scraper, 11. Flake blade 12. Notch scrapers, 13. Flutted cores, 14. Blades, 15. Burins, 16. Lunates, 17. Celt

Figure 2. Stone tool assemblage from Shigarh site

The vegetation of this area includes Sal (*Shorea robusta*), Kendu (*Diospyros melanoxylon*), Kusum (*Schleichera sylvestris*), Tamarind (*Tamarindus indica*), and Mango (*Mangifera indica*). Among these Sal is the dominant plant with various flowering trees and thorny bushes distributed in this region. Both tribal and non-tribal people are living in this area. The tribals include mostly Juang, Sabaras, Bhumij, Kishan, Ho, Munda, Bhuian and others. A continuing sequence of Lower Paleolithic to Neolithic habitation has been identified in stratified sections. Rich forest produces, raw materials and nearby water sources attracted people to inhabit the place since prehistoric times (Figure 2).

Cultural assemblage

The cultural assemblage shows the Chrono cultural sequence of Stone Age from Palaeolithic to Neolithic period. The Palaeolithic implements are primarily core bifaces with some flake tools. The frequency of hand axes was dominant over chopper and cleaver. Hand axes show typo-technological development from Block-on Block technique to Cylinder hammer technique. Scrapers are predominant tools. Different types of scrapers have been found i.e. Single sided scrapers (19.67%), Double sided scrapers (19.67%), Side cum end scrapers (32.79%), End scrapers (4.92%) and Notch scrapers (22.95%). Other flake tools are point, knife and flake blade. Blades, burin and awls were also found. Flake tools are made on both Clactonian and Levalloisian flake. Tools made by Levalloisian technology are predominant over Clactonian technology. Raw materials used for making tools are primarily quartzite and quartz.

The Mesolithic deposition comprises of cores (29.12%), flakes (37.78%) and microliths (33.10%). These assemblages prove that the site is a factory site. Microliths are made on both flake (46%) and blade (54%). Side scrapers, end scrapers, round scrapers, side cum end scrapers, thumbnail scrapers, notch scrapers, keeled scrapers, points are made on flake whereas backed blades, burins, lunate, trapeze are made on blades. Fluting technique was prevalent during the Mesolithic period. They used mostly quartz, quartzite, chert were for making tools. Neolithic assemblages are found on the Mesolithic layer, sometimes combined with the microliths. Celts, chisel is common polished tools with the evidences of hand made and wheel made potsherds. Red ware was predominant. Dolerite was primary raw material suitable for making polished tools. Extensive exploration may unfold many hidden factors for continuation of prehistoric habitation. There is number of caves in surrounding hilly areas. The site preserves not only the cultural remains but also the cultural land scape. Site has number of possibilities to become a heritage site.

Site Kuanr in Keonjhar district of Odisha

The site was first discovered by Ray (1993) situated on the north-west of the NH-6 near the culvert No 378 in Keonjhar district of Odisha. The site is on the mound (600 m above the sea level) and naturally fortified by nullah, tributaries of the river Baitarini. The area is surrounded by hilly forest. Rich forest resources, nearby sources of water and raw materials for making stone tools, metal ores attracted people for habitation. Clay was also locally available for making pottery. Chalcolithic habitation has been found on the Holocene deposition over the ghutin layer. The clay is lateritic in nature. The site is presently used for agricultural purpose.

Cultural Assemblages

The Several seasons of exploration and trial digging have been carried out, which yielded stone tools, pot shreds, terracotta and metal objects. Flake tool comprises different types of scrapers, points, awls, borers, knives and microliths. The Neolithic tool types are axes, adzes, sickles, ring stone and saddle querns. The evidence of raw materials, cores, flakes, finished and unfinished tools suggest that the site was used both for habitation purpose as well as factory site. It was also used for habitation purpose as well as different aspects of early metallurgy. Raw materials used for making tools are altered basalt with quartz and chert.

A large number of metal objects have been found. These comprise bangles of different sizes and designs, rings, pendants, amulets and small bell with dark green patina. A necklace of carnelian beads has been found with brass pendants. Archaeo-metallurgical analysis suggests that these were very old type brass, alloy of copper, zinc and tin. The alloy contains 33% of zinc with 54% of copper and small amount of tin (8.5%) and other impurities (Ray *et al.* 2000). The alloy was produced by the simultaneous reduction of chalcopyrite and Pb-Zn sulphide ore by charcoal. The ornaments were produced by lost wax process. It has immense importance in the understanding of the emergence and development of brass technology in Eastern India and its diffusion towards the different parts of the Indian subcontinent (Figure 3).

Destruction of the sites

Above description shows the rich cultural heritage of prehistoric period in Odisha. The sites are being destroyed by number of reasons day by day. The agents of destruction are primarily two- natural agents and Human agents. Human agents are two types- incidental, which involved agriculture, land clearing, grazing, and construction of road, water management etc. and intentional causes are archaeological exploration and excavation, looting, vandalism (Nickens, 1991). In the present case both the sites are victims of natural destruction. Vegetation cover and soil layer play as a protective

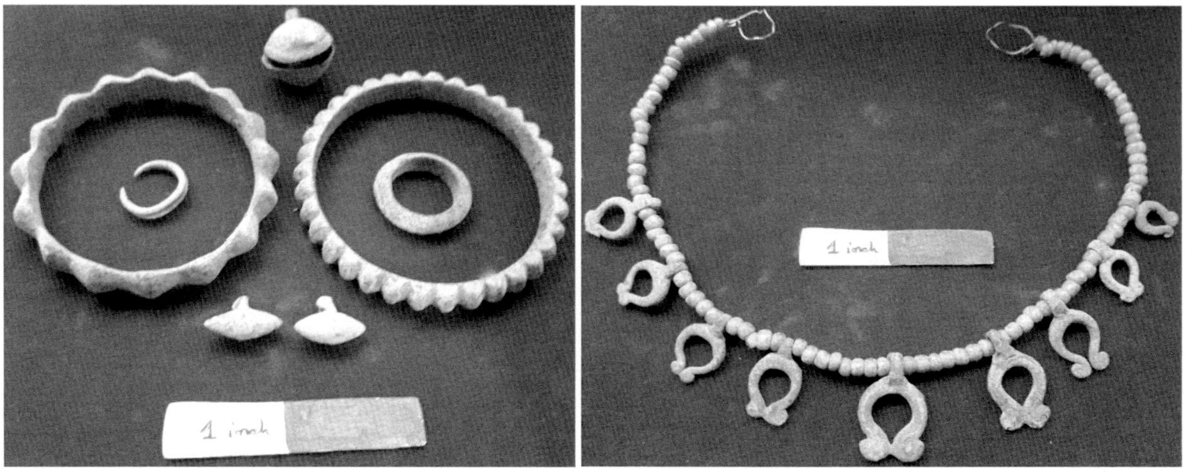

Figure 3. Metal remains of site Kuanr

buffer between the atmosphere and the earth's crust. In humid condition, taller plants break raindrop and prevent the direct rain splash on soil. The natural plants are completely or partially removed due to number of reasons like deforestation, field clearance, burning of grass land, animal grazing and agriculture. The shrubs covering most of the areas of Kuanr are brunt by local people for clearing the lands for agriculture. These result in soil loosening. Cultivation process include digging, hoeing, ploughing. Grazing of animals also loosened exposed soil. Due to the felling of trees and cutting of shrubs the organic matter is rapidly oxidized in the sun and allows lesser water to absorb during rainy season tends to soil erosion. Agriculture is a regular activity in the Kuanr and Shigarh area. Soil erosion is highly accelerated at Kuanr site due to forest clearing for cultivation.

The southern side of the mound Kuanr is very steep forming a gorge. Earlier the gorge was covered up by jungle. But due to the deforestation the erosional activity of soil increased during the rainy season and this gorge is expanding day by day. The mound is surrounded by nullah in its three sides. These sides are also very cliff and erosional activity is very high. So, it is observed during the field exploration that the destruction due to erosion is rampant in the site Kuanr (Figure 4 and figure 5).

Figure 4. Destruction of site Kuanr

Figure 5. Destruction of site Shigarh

The agent of erosion does not only play destruction activity, but also collect and transport the loose materials. Gully formations also have been observed in the studied area. Gullies are formed due to cutting down the underlying floor at different depths due to the flow of water. Small gullies are joined and form a larger one. The direction of flow is towards the depressed area from the elevated region.

In most of the cases the artefacts collected from the different prehistoric sites are preserved and displayed in the museums. These collections are helpful to know the typology and evolution of artefacts rather than the cultural landscape. So the priority should be given to preserve the artefacts *in situ* position. Natural erosion can be minimized by proper planning and long-term management programme. Public awareness also has an important role for protecting the sites. In the present case local people are ignorant about the value of the artefacts which have been found around the sites. If they are aware of the value properly they would help to preserve the sites and heritage.

Conclusion

It is clear from the above literatures that except for a very few exceptions the prehistoric sites are not considered very seriously under the purview of heritage management in India in general and Odisha in particular. The cultural remains of the past are so valuable that these could not be renewed. The prehistoric sites are mainly found in remote areas and not easily accessible. As for example cliff slopes of the mountain, forest and top of the hill. Caves are also acquired by predators at present. Most of the sites are explored. Surrounding areas are not circumscribed and are used for agricultural land and grazing purpose. It is pre-eminently a cultural phenomenon linked to de-vegetation and destruction of the organic topsoil by cultivation or over intensive grazing. Within a few generations, or even a few years, such accelerated soil erosion can change surface forms and move more soil as well as cultural remains. Loosening of top soil is caused by deforestation. Rootless soil is highly eroded by small rainfall. On the other hand, most of the protected sites are now of an easy access to all; both men and animals. The sites sometimes were used for recreation. In conclusion, it may be said that governments; both the state and the central should come forward to undertake different projects to protect our cultural heritage, which is also our identity. Campaigning among the local people in this area about the importance of the place will help to make local people aware of the great heritage. It can be assumed from the above discussion that the prehistoric sites and cultural remains should be preserved.

References

Acharya, P. (1923-24) – *Annual Report of the Archeological Survey of India*, pp. 100-101.
Banerji, R. D. (1930) – *History of Orissa*, Vol. I. Calcutta: Prabasi Press.

Ball, V. (1876) – On Stone implements found in the tributary states of Orissa, *Proceedings of the Asiatic Society of Bengal*, pp. 120-121.

Basa, K. K. (1984) – *Prehistory of Mayurbhanj: A Review*, Unpublished M.A. Dissertation, Utkal University, Bhubaneswar.

Basa, K. K. and B. Mohanta (1999) – Stone Age Cultures Around Burla, Western Orissa, Orissa. *Historical Research Journal*, XLIII (No 14). pp. 13-26.

Basa, K. K., T. K. Das & B. K. Mohanta (2000) – Neolithic Culture of Pallahara, Central Orissa. In Basa and Mohanty (ed.) *Archeology of Orissa*. Delhi: Pratibha Prakashan. pp. 264-284.

Behera, P. K. (1989) – *Archaeology of Sundargarh District with special Reference to the Brahmani valley, Orissa*. Unpublished Ph. D Thesis, Varanasi: Banaras Hindu University.

Behera, P. K. (1992) – Sulabhdihi: A Neolithic Celt Manufacturing Centre in Orissa, *Puratattva* 22: 124-132.

Behera, P. K. (2000) – Neolithic Culture Complex of Bonaigarh, Orissa. In Basa and Mohanty (ed.) *Archeology of Orissa*. Delhi: Pratibha Prakashan.pp. 222-263.

Behera, P. K. (2006) – Investigations into the Mesolithic and Post-Mesolithic Settlements in the Middle Mahanadi Valley, Orissa. In S. Pradhan (ed.) *Art and Archeology of Orissa: Recent Perspectives*, New Dehi: Aryan Book Internationa.

Behera, P. K. (2013) – New Light on the Neolithic and Chalcolithic Evidence from the Middle Mahanadi Valley, Orissa. In K. N. Dikshit (ed.) *Neolithic-Chalcolithic Cultures of Eastern India*. New Delhi: Indian Archeological Society, Special Report No. 5. pp. 184-207.

Behera, P. K., P. Panda and N. Thakur (1996) – Techno-typological Analysis of Lithic Artefacts from the Dari-Dangri Acheulian site, Sambalpur District, Orissa. *Man and Environment*. 21(2): 15-26.

Bhatt, S.C. (2008) – *The Encyclopedic District Gazetteers of India*, Eastern Zone (Vol. 9). Gyan publishing House, New Delhi.

Bose, N. K. and D. Sen (1948) – *Excavation in Mayurbhanj*. Calcutta: Calcutta University.

Chakraborty, D. K. (1993) – *Archeology of Eastern India: Chhota Nagpur Plateau and West Bengal*. New Delhi: Munsiram Monoharlal.

Chakrabarti, S. (1990) – The stone age prehistory of Khiching, Orissa. *Man and Environment* 15: 13-21.

Chakrabarti, S. (2000) – Recent Advances in Prehistory of Mayurbhanj. In Basa and Mohanty (ed.) *Archeology of Orissa*. Delhi: Pratibha Prakashan. pp. 77-101.

Dash, R. N. (2000) – The Neolithic Culture of Orissa: A Typo-technological Analysis. In Basa and Mohanty (ed.) *Archeology of Orissa*. Delhi: Pratibha Prakashan. pp. 201-221.

Indian Archaeology Review (1956-57) – *Archaeological Survey of India*: New Delhi.

Kar, S. K. (1995-96) – Further Exploration at Gopalpur, Orissa, *Puratattva* 26: 105-106.

Kar, S. K. (2000) – Gopalpur: A Neolithic-Chalcolithic Site in Coastal Orissa. In Basa and Mohanty (ed.) *Archeology of Orissa*. Delhi: Pratibha Prakashan. pp. 368-391.

Lal, B. B. (1953) – Protohistoric investigation. *Ancient India* 9: 97.

Majumder, N. D. (1955) – Some prehistoric finds in Orissa. *Proceedings of the 42nd Indian Science Congress*, Pt, III, Section VIII:321.

Mishra, S. K. (1982-83) – Stone Age Antiquities of Sarasara and Other Sites in the Jira River-Basin of Orissa: A Reappraisal, *Manav* I: 31-42.

Mishra, S. K. (1990) – Stone Age Remains and Palaeo-human activities in the Burhabalang and Chipat river valleys of Orissa, *Man in Society*, 4: 21-33.

Mohanta, B. K. (2001) – *Neolithic and Post Neolithic cultures of Northern Orissa*. Unpublished Ph. D thesis, Utkal University, Bhubaneswar.

Mohanty, P. (1989) – Mesolithic Settlement System of Keonjhar District, Orissa, *Man in India*. 77 (2 & 3): 159-77.

Mohanty, P. (2000) – Mesolithic Culture and Ethnography of Keonjhar District, Orissa. In Basa and Mohanty (ed.) *Archaeology of Orissa*. Delhi: Pratibha Prakashan. pp. 114-152.

Mohanty, P. (1992) – Stone Age research in Orissa: An overview. *Man in India* 72, No. 2: 207-32.

Mohanty, P., K. K. Basa and B. Tripathy (1997) – Stone Age Cultures of Mayurbhanj District, Orissa, *Man in India* 77 (2 & 3): 159-77.

Mohapatra, G. C. (1962) – *The Stone Age Cultures of Orissa*. Poona: Deccan College.

Nanda, S. C. (1982-83) – A Note on Stone Age Succession of Indravati Valley, Koraput district, Orissa. *Manav* 1 (1): 83-5.

Nanda, S. C. (1984) – *Stone Age Cultures of Indravati Valley, District Koraput, Orissa*, Unpublished Ph. D Thesis, Pune: University of Pune.

Nickens, P. R. (1991) – The destruction of archeological sites and data. In G. S. Smith and J. E. Ehrenhard (eds.) *Protecting the Past*, Boca Raton, Florida: CRC Press, Inc.

Ota, S. B. (1986) – Mesolithic Culture of the Phulbani district (Orissa) with Special Reference to the heavy Tool Component. *Bulletin of Deccan College Post Graduate and Research Institute*. 45: 47-56.

Ratha, S. N. & D. K. Bhattacharya (1988) – Lower Palaeolithic from Kuchinda (Orissa). *Man and Environment*, 12: 23-8.

Pustry, R. P. (1972) – A note on celt from Koraput. *Adibasi*, 14, No 2: 67-70.

Ratha, S. N. and D. K. Bhattacharya (1988) – Lower Palaeolithic from Kuchinda (Orissa). *Man and Environment*, 12: 23-8.

Ray, R. (1993) – Discovery of a Chalcolithic site near the source of river Baitarini, Orissa. *Journal of the Indian Anthropological Society*, 28 (1): 97-102.

Ray, R. (1996) – Some observation on the prehistoric sites in the vicinity of Pallahara Township, Orissa. In N. K. Behura & K. C. Tripathy (ed.) *Biocultural Frontiers in Anthropology*. Mittal Publications, New Delhi.

Ray, R., A. K. Kundu & N. Bhattacharya (2000) – Chalcolithic Cultural remains from a Site near Kanjipani, Orissa. In Basa and Mohanty (ed.) *Archeology of Orissa*. Delhi: Pratibha Prakashan. pp. 356-367.

Ray, R. & D. K. Mondal (2013) – Chalco-Neolithic Culture of Eastern India with a focus on the findings from the site Kuanr, Keonjhar, Orissa. In K. N. Dikshit (ed.) *Neolithic-Chalcolithic Cultures of Eastern India*. New Delhi: Indian Archeological Society, Special Report No. 5. 111-118.

Roy, S. (2011) – *The Story of Indian Archeology 1784-1947*. New Delhi: Archeological Survey of India. pp. 53-54.

Sahoo (1987-88) – *Stone Age Industries of Darpan Khas, Cuttack*, Unpublished M. Phil dissertation, Bhubaneswar: Utkal University.

Sahoo, D. & K. K. Basa (2013) – Neolithic and Chalcolithic Cultures of Odisha: An Overview. In K. N. Dikshit (ed.) *Neolithic-Chalcolithic Cultures of Eastern India*. New Delhi: Indian Archeological Society, Special Report No. 5. pp. 173-183.

Sen, D., G. S. Ray & A. Beteille (1956) – A New Paleolithic Site in Mayurbhanj. *Man in India*. Vol. 36, no-4, pp. 233-246.

Sharma, H. C. (1994) – Palaeolithic Finds around Burla, District Sambalpur, Orissa. *Man and Environment* 19 (1 & 2): 285-90.

Singh, P. K. (1985) – *Prehistory of Central Orissa*, Unpublished Ph.D. Thesis, Bhubaneswar: Utkal University.

Singh, P. K. (1988) – Cultural succession of prehistoric culture in central Orissa. In K. L. Bhowmick (ed.) *Culture of the Past*. New Delhi: inter India publication. pp. 87-99.

Sinha, B. K. (1990-91) – Excavation at Golbai Sasan, Dist. Puri, Orissa. *Puratattva* 21: 74-76.

Sinha, B. K. (2000) – Golbai: A Protohistoric Site on the Coast of Orissa, In Basa and Mohanty (ed.) *Archeology of Orissa*. Delhi: Pratibha Prakashan. pp. 322-355.

Sinha, B. K. (1988-89) – Neolithic Culture of Central Orissa, *Manav* 3: pp. 275-81.

Tripathy, K. C. (1966) – A metric study of the Neolithic celts of Mayurbhanj, *Orissa Historical research Journal*, Vol. 14, No. 2: 13-20.

Tripathy, K. C. (1972) – *Lithic Industries of Southwestern Orissa*. Unpublished Ph. D Thesis, Utkal University, Orissa.

Tripathy, K. C. (1980) – *Lithic industries in India: A Study of South Western Orissa*. New Delhi: Inter India Publication.

Tripathy, K. C. (1982-83) – Preliminary Archeological Survey of the 1b, *Manav* 1 (1): 60-66.

Swain, N. K. and D. N. Bhoi (2010) – New light on prehistoric Archeology of Middle Brahmani valley, Central Orissa. *Proceedings of the National Seminar on Archeology of Chhattisgarh and latest Excavation at Pachrahi*; 185-200.

Thapar, B. K. (1985) – *Recent Archeological Discoveries in India*, Paris: UNESCO.

Yule, P., B. K. Rath, K. Hojgaard (1989) – Sankerjang- ein metallzeitlicher Beststtungsplatzim Dhenkanal-Vorgebirge ostindiens, *Anthropos* 84: 107-132.

Yule, P. & B. K. Rath (2000) – Sankerjang-A Metal Period Burial Site in the Dhenkanal Uplands of Orissa. In Basa and Mohanty (ed.) *Archeology of Orissa*. Delhi: Pratibha Prakashan. pp. 285-321.

Worman, E. C. (Jr.), (1949) – The Neolithic problem in the prehistory of India. *Journal of the Washington Academy of Science*, 39, No 6: 181-201.

Heritage of skill in making clay ornaments in India

Koyel Chakraborty
Junior Research Fellow; Anthropological Survey of India
kchakraborty88@gmail.com

Debasis Kumar Mondal
Assistant Professor; Department of Anthropology, Calcutta University
anth.debasis@gmail.com

Ranjana Ray
Professor Emeritus; Department of Anthropology, Calcutta University
prof.ranjana.ray@gmail.com

Abstract
Personal adornment is very common feature among human beings. Ornaments have been found from archaeological sites in India even before the onset of Indus valley civilization. Present work is on terracotta ornaments with focus on bangles. Bangles found from Harappan culture is analysed and compared with present day types. Terracotta bangles have a long history of existence in India. The making of bangles needs special skill not only for the manufacturing process but also the choice of raw material, technique of firing and decorating. Present paper deals with this tangible and intangible cultural heritage of India with understanding of continuity of cultural traits.

Key words
Intagible, tangible, heritage, terracotta, Bangles, manufacture, continuity, craft and craftsmen

Introduction

Ornament is a form of personal adornment comprises of necklaces, rings, bangles, earrings etc. may be made from any material natural or artificial. The natural materials include clay, wood, horn, bone, shell, ivory, flowers, wild berries, leaves and feathers, precious metals, gemstones etc. It bears a number of functional aspects including ritualistic, status symbol, superstitious beliefs and concepts.

Present focus is given on terracotta ornaments. Natural clay contains different minerals and colouring oxides. Prepared clay are moulded, modeled and then dried; after firing it became a perishable object. The earliest terracotta objects in the form of pottery and figurines found in India, Egypt and Mesopotemia (Sengupta, 2005).

Terracotta ornaments may have been originated because of easily availability of raw materials. The craft originated, flourished and became a part of social life of people with the other ornaments made from different raw materials. Kenoyer (1991), made a comparative study of social ranking of the ornaments found in Archaeological sites in India particularly in case of Harappan civilization. Terracotta ornaments were made from common and locally available clay and made by relative simple technology, they were considered as of the lowest rank and worn by the people who belong to the lowest social ranking. On the other hand, shell, unfired steatite and other stone beads made from exotic raw materials and are used by the middle-ranked people, but beads made of precious materials, such as, fired steatite, faience, carnelian, copper, which required complex technologies were of the highest rank. Similarly, the artisans who worked on gold and carnelian might have been ranked higher than those who made terracotta ornaments. The evidences of terracotta beads and bangles have been found from Prehistoric period. The craft of flourished during Chalcolithic and

Early Historic period. Large numbers of Terracotta bangles were found from Harappan sites. Many of the terracotta bangles were originally painted with black or red designs. (Kenoyer, 1991). At present terracotta ornaments are used as exotic fashion jewellery. It has demand in the society for ethnic look, different and cheaper than the other ornaments and the demand of wearing terracotta ornaments are increasing day by day. The products include necklaces, earrings, bracelets, bangles, danglers and pendants etc.

Objectives and methodology

Study of technology of terracotta ornament has immense importance to understand the technology of the past. Traditionally common motifs and designs are important clue to understand the diffusion, exchange and trade. The present focus is not only given to the reconstruction of indigenous technology of making terracotta ornament but on the status of these objects in the society and the survivality of the craft in present day. In the sense of fundamental the terracotta ornaments of prehistoric and modern time have much difference but similarities have been found in respect to materials, technology, forms and function. Good deals of modification have been made in skill of design, colouring, diversities and function in accordance with needs.

The present study has been done in different parts of the state of West Bengal, in Eastern India. Also different markets have been surveyed for price, diversity, supply, marketing of terracotta ornaments and ritualistic aspects attached with this craft. There is an attempt to know the particular social situation in which the craft is continuing. In addition to technology, other related matters such as labour, availability or raw materials, order, supply of finished products and other problems related to the craft have been taken into account. Standard Anthropological methodology is used for the present study. Methods used are mainly Observation, direct interview through both structured and structured schedule.

Skill in making the terracotta ornaments

Making of terracotta objects is old and traditional in nature. In the present study data have been collected on raw material, sources of clay and fuel, tools used, process of making of ornaments, mode of firing, finishing and finally marketing of products. Basic raw materials necessary for pottery making is clay with other materials like paddy husk, fuel, water. Colour is also used to decorate the ornaments. Artisans in the area recognize the quality of the clay from its colour and texture. The artisans inherit the knowledge of the generations. For various types of ornaments the craftsmen used to prepare the clay by mixing in various proportions of different clays and paddy husk. Paddy husk is used as tempering material. For fuel, cow dung cake and coal are used. Other materials needed are mustard oil, brass strings, lace and different waterproof colours.

Raw materials needed for making terracotta ornaments

Development of terracotta as a craft usually depends on the availability of the suitable raw materials. Basic raw materials necessary for pottery making is clay. Other secondary raw materials are fuel, water. Colour is also used to decorate the ornaments.

- Clay: Artisans in the area recognise the quality of the clay from its colour and texture. They prepare five types of clay to make different coloured ornaments.
- Orange Clay: Orange coloured clay is produced by mixing of alluvial clay of the river Ganges with lateritic clay and clay from cultivated land. These are mixed in equal proportion (1:1:1) and 1/3 proportion china clay is also mixed with that to produce orange colour.
- White Clay: White clay is a mixture of slime clay of pond, chalk and clayey soil in an equal proportion. China clay also is mixed up with this preparation in 1/3 proportion.
- Black Clay: This clay is of preparation of alluvium of the river Ganges and Clayey soil in 1:1 proportion.

- Sandal Wood Coloured Clay: This is a mixture of clayey soil, alluvium of the river Ganges and chalk in equal proportion.
- Brown Coloured Clay: This coloured clay is produced by mixing of lateritic clay, alluvium of the river Ganges and china clay in 1:1:1 proportion.

Tools and appliances

Implements which are used in making ornaments are classified according to their functions.

Implements for Cutting

- Cutter: These are made of aluminium sheet used by hand. The working edge is concave or straight used for cutting different designs. Mainly concave cutters are used to cut and remove excess parts of rounded ornaments and the straight cutters are used to remove straight part of the ornaments. These are varying in size. Length varies from 2 cm. to 4.5 cm. Breadth also varies from 0.4 cm. to 2 cm.
- Knife: Iron knife also used to cut and remove the excess parts of the ornaments. The working end is sharp and pointed. This is made from iron blade. The cutting edge is at the anterior part of the tool obliquely set with two lateral margins of the tool.

Tools for Designing and Decoration

Different tools are used to make different designs. These are either made of wood or from other raw materials. Some tools are also made from disposable materials.

- Impression Pen: This tool is made of wood. Mainly wood of guava tree is used for making this pen. This has square cross section. The working end is produced by scraping of wood. This is made by them. This tool is used to make straight longitudinal incised lines. Length of the tool is 13.5 cm. The maximum circumference of the tool is 4 cm.
- Punch: These are used for punching different designs from ornaments. The cross sections are of different. These are used for punching different designs such as small circles, petals and triangles. These are mainly made of aluminium. The puncher with big circumference is used to make big holes and the puncher with comparatively small circumference is used to make small holes. The length varies from 6 cm to 8 cm. There is a handle made of jute and adhesive for easy hand hold and prevent slipperiness at the time of punching.
- Moulds: Different moulds are used to incise different designs on clay ornaments. These are mainly made of aluminium sheet. For petal design the moulds vary in length from 2.8 cm to 5.5 cm. the breadth varies from 1.5 cm to 2.7 cm. The oval mould made of aluminium of 10.2 cm in breadth and 4 cm in length is used to make hair clip. Mould with circular cross section is used to make round designs known as 'til'. Eye shaped moulds also used which are elongated rectangular in shape.

Wooden piston, earthen plate, one half of a cricket ball is used for giving shape of ornaments:

- Wooden Table: A table made from teak wood (*Tectona grandis*). Its length is 40 cm and breadth is 30 cm. the table is 25 cm high. It has four legs. At the top of the table three sides are covered by wooden borders. One side is open. Designs of ornaments are done on top of the table. Instruments also are kept there.
- Needle: It is an iron rod of 8 cm in length. The one end is curved and another end is straight. These are used to make small holes in beads to tie up the strings for hanging.
- Pliers: Iron pliers are small pincers with farm straight jaws used for bending and cutting metal strings. The length is 13 cm.
- Iron Snipers: This is a very useful tool designed to perform all the major cuttings of aluminium sheets. The length is 15 cm. the handles are made of plastic.

- Iron Disc: Iron disc is used to fix the iron strings for hanging of beads. It has 7 cm. diameters. The height is 2 cm. There is a hole at the center.
- Magnet: A piece of magnet is used to fix up the bent iron strings.
- Wooden Roller: A wooden roller is used to make circular clay slab. This is brought from market. It is cylindrical in shape. There are two handles at the two ends of the implement. The length is 40 cm. and the medial circumference is 12 cm. the handle is 8 cm in circumference
- Brush: Brushes of different shape and sizes are used to paint the ornaments. These are bought from Kolkata.
- Cotton Cloth: A cotton cloth square in shape is used to keep processes clay or unfinished ornaments.

Tools Used for Firing

Earthen Pot

It is wide mouthed earthen pot used for colouring black ornaments at the time of firing. The circumference of mouth is 75 cm. The medium circumference is 80 cm. The height of the pot is 72 cm. This was bought from local market.

Stages of Production of Ornaments

Broadly speaking the main stages of manufacture of terracotta ornaments can be divided into four main stages: Preparation of clay, Shaping, Designing, Drying, Firing, Painting and Finishing of the ornaments.

Preparation of Clay

Actual manufacturing of ornaments is started with the preparation of clay. After collection, the clay is beaten and the grits are picked up and impurities are taken out by hand. It is taken of one hour to prepare of 10 kg clay. The cleaned clay is soaked in water for 30 to 45 days. The different types of clay are soaked in different container. Then the clay is further sieved of impurities by mosquito net. Then the cleaned clay is further soaked after mixing of different proportion of clay for different colour for one month to three months. It will be easier to form the ornaments when it is well soaked for several months. Moist clay dries more rapidly on the outer surface which is exposed to air, with the result that the moisture content is not uniform throughout the clay mass. Therefore, before modelling the clay it is necessary that it be kneaded to mix all parts thoroughly. Before the modelling the soaked clay is kept in an air tight box for twenty days. Then Clay is kneaded by both hands. Water is added to the clay at regular intervals. Air bubbles may be present in the clay and must be wedged out. If the clay is too much moist and sticky to the fingers it will collapse during and after modelling. Kneading brings the whole mass of clay to a uniform consistency of water and clay. After proper kneading, the clay is ready for modelling. Clay for ceramic ornaments is generally worked into thin piece, so it is essential that the clay be kept fairly moist and workable all the times. Plastic clay not in use should be stored in a bucket or earthen ware pot with a lid, to seal the air and prevent the clay for dying out. Partially modelled clay, upon which it is desired to continue work later, should be completely covered with a moist cloth or air tight container to retain the moisture in the clay.

Shaping of the Ornaments

Different methods are applied for making different ornaments as described below. Sometimes more than one method is used to shape single ornament.

Slab Method

Required amount of clay is again kneaded by fingers to make sure that the clay has no grit. Then the clay is flattened with the palm of the hands until it forms a round shape about 1/8-inches-thick. Then it is placed on a smooth surface and sometimes on newspaper and rolled with the roller until the disc is quite thin about 1/8-inch-thick and even in all area. Then it is tested by knife either is it even or uneven. Different types of moulds are used for shaping different ornaments. Different shapes are cut with different moulds. Clay ornaments are removed from the slab one by one with the help of knife and fingers of hand.

Shaping of the ornaments

These are again shaped in moulds. As for example hair clip are shaped on a mould of earthen. This structure looks like concave-convex shape. The rounded pendants also moulded in half cricket ball to give the earthen lid (concavo-convex) shape. Different shaped pendants, hair clip and ear rings etc. are produced by this method.

Coiling Method

Bangles are mainly produced by this method. Small proportion of kneaded clay is taken and a round sticks about 6-inch-long and 2 inches in diameter is prepared. Rolling is done back and forth under the palms. Light, quick, back and forth motion is applied with the palms. At frequent intervals fingers are dipped in a bowl of water. Then a steel glass is taken. Little amount of mustard oil is smeared at the edge of the glass with brush. Then the stick is bent rounding the edge of the glass until both ends touch each other. If the clay is too wet the circle will collapse. If the clay is too dry, cracks will appear at the outside of the circle. Then two ends are cut at a long slant and sum incised marks done with knife. Then two ends are joined together and smoothened the surface with water by soft brush.

Moulding Method (Figure 1)

Moulding is one of the simple method used for making terracotta beads. Two pieces of mould of plaster of Paris are covered with prepared clay with pressure of fingers. Then these two moulds are joined together and the beads get their shape. After pressing the moulds are opened.

Hand moulding

They are also expert of shaping of ornaments by fingers and hands. Probably this is the earliest method of shaping terracotta ornaments. Hair pins, bell shaped ear rings, beads are prepared by hands.

Beads

Beads are produced by circular motion applied by two palms of the hands. Clay is rounded with clockwise motion of palms.

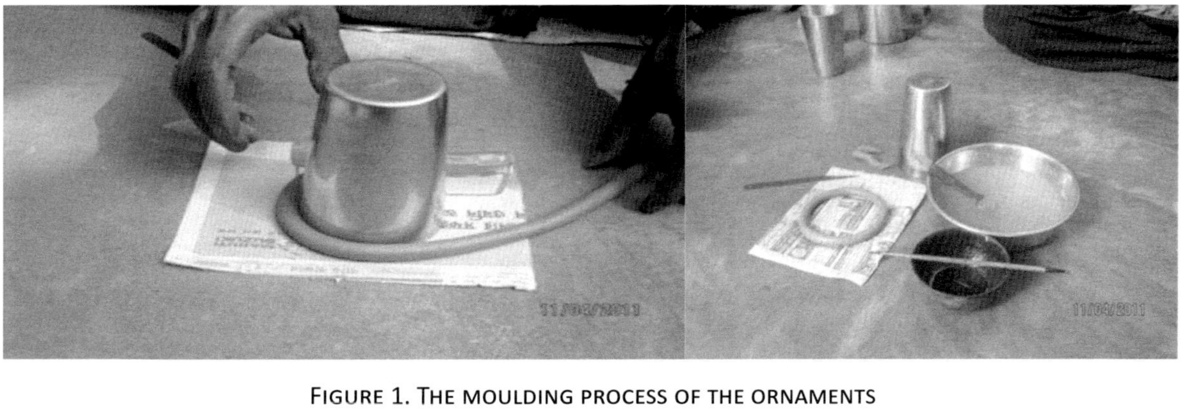

Figure 1. The moulding process of the ornaments

Ear rings

This is made of barrel shaped beads. These beads are cut into two equal halves. Different designs are incised on the rings. Then the inner portion is scoop out with knife.

Hair pin

Small wedged clay is taken at first. Then the shape petals are formed with the fingers by turning them up. The leaves are gently rolled to give them natural shape. These petals are assembled one by one from the inner to outer portion with a stick. The inner petals are small and outer petals are comparatively bigger.

Designing of the Ornaments (Figure 2)

Designing is an important aspect of any craft to make different and choice able. At first, ornamentation took the form of 'scratching' or 'incising' the surface of the object. Incising means literally 'to cut into', and was performed by sharpened wooden sticks, stone knife or bone instrument. There are two types or designs found in terracotta ornaments – Plastic decoration and painting. Only plastic decoration is done before firing. The plastic form of decoration is usually accomplished while the clay is pliable. This form includes the incising, impressing, embossing etc. These are done by simple tools mentioned earlier.

Drying of the Ornaments (Figure 2)

The ornaments completed are thoroughly dried in the sun. The smaller ornaments are dried for two to three days and comparatively bigger ornaments take six to seven days for drying. At first these are dried in shade and finally in direct sun. In rainy season, these are dried under the lamp.

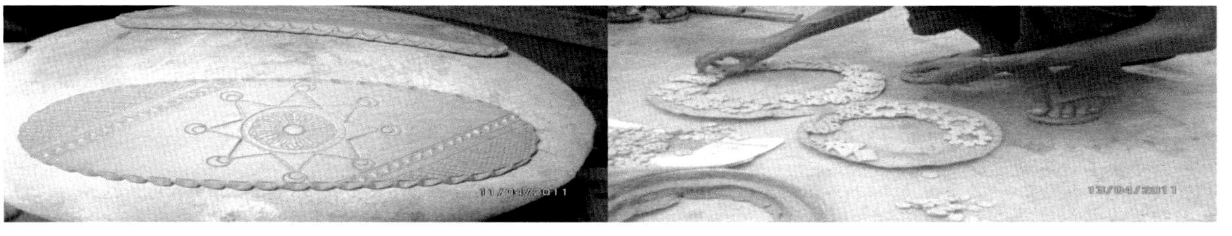

FIGURE 2. DESIGN AND DRYING PROCESS OF THE ORNAMENTS

Firing (Figure 3)

Firing is usually started at noon. Firing is done in several stages. At first cow dung cake is arranged on the iron rods in the kiln. Then chunk of charcoal is broken into small pieces by hammering. Then the coal is covered from the stoke holes. These are ignited with kerosene spreader over the ash from the bottom of the kiln. Fully dried ornaments are arranged on iron ring plate which has hole in the centre. Three plates with ornaments are placed one after one in decrease towards the end. At the middle, there is a net which is also filled with dried ornaments. When the fire raised ornaments started to bake. Firing in reduced oxidation is done to get the black colour. Paddy husk is spread in a wide mouthed earthen pot. The ornaments are also covered with husk in the pot. One pot is covered with another pot. After heating in reduced condition, the colour becomes black.

As their statement maturing point of different types of clay used by them as follows:

Types of Clay	Maturing Temperature
Black	6000 C to 7000 C
Orange	6000 C to 6500 C
Pink	6500 C to 7000 C
Red	6000 C to 6500 C

TABLE 1. THE TIME TAKEN FOR FIRING IS ABOUT ONE HOUR. THEN THE FIRED ORNAMENTS ARE TAKEN OUT WITH PINCERS COOLED

Painting and Finishing of the ornaments (Figure 3)

All ornaments are not painted. Paintings are done after firing of ornaments. Different fabric paints are applied with soft brush. In the present work two families are studied out of them one family used to paint their ornaments and another left the ornaments natural colour. The technology of finishing the ornaments of second family is different from the first. They also produce different shaped small and loose ornamental designs. After firing these are fixed with adhesive according to designs. Finishing of ornaments is generally done by women. The adjustment of the lace with the pendants, joining of different parts, fastening bar pins, ear screws and ear clip are done at final stage. Then these finished products are put in transparent packets and ready for the market. Delivery is done after packaging.

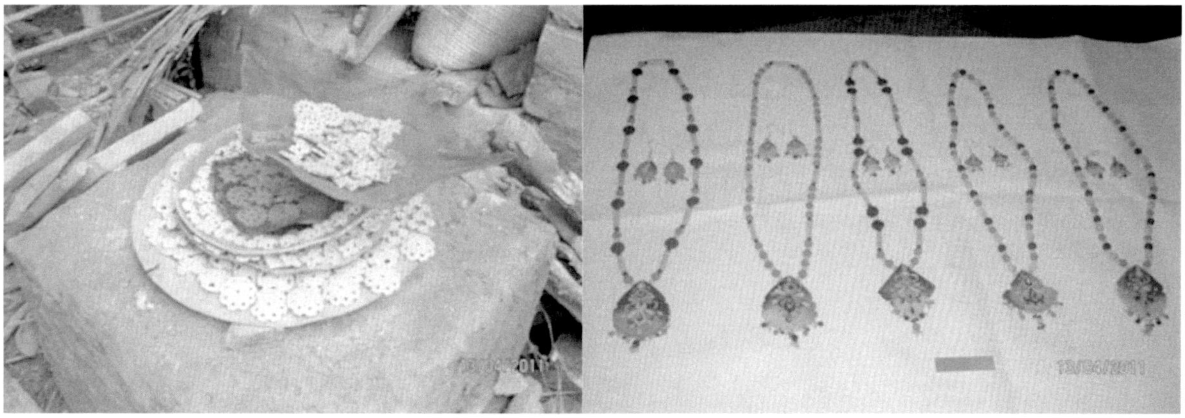

FIGURE 3. THE FIRING PROCESS OF THE ORNAMENTS, AND THE FINAL RESULTS

Storage, Marketing and Transport

Storage is essential and indispensible only when there is a time gap between the production and disposal of products. The artisans keep their finished products in store for some time they generally store them in their room for safety and protection. Finished ornaments are packed in decorative plastic bags. A trunk made of tin used as container. The finished products are packed by transparent and stored in the box. The finished products are delivered to their order supplier. Artisans use private buses and train for delivery of finished item.

Production and Price

The three main products which have regular demand are bangles, ear rings, necklace and pendants. There are also many items such as terracotta hair pin, wrist band etc. Prices are also varied in different places such as market and fair. The different items have different prices according to shape and sizes. There is also a seasonal variation of demand of products.

Conclusion

Terracotta ornaments have decorative value, social status, and economic position, ritualistic value from prehistoric and protohistoric period. Large number of terracotta bangles were found from Harappan sites. Many of the terracotta bangles were originally painted with black or red designs. It involved special type of clay mixed with tempering material kneaded with water. The stages include rolling out clay sheets, cutting into shapes, moulding, drying and firing, then decorating. Craft is our cultural heritage. The craft is practiced in household. As a household craft, the family members are engaged in different stages of production. Both males and females are involved in the stages of production. It needs skill, knowledge and became a part of our cultural heritage. It has a tangible cultural heritage and intangible part is also involved with it. The craft survived because of rituals and beliefs attached to it. It is revived for aesthetics. Efforts are being for sustainable development of the crafts and craftsmen.

References

Kenoyer, J. M. (1991) – Ornament Style of the Indus valley Tradition: Evidence from recent excavation at Harappa, Pakistan. *Paleorient*, Vol 17/2.

Sengupta, A. R. (2005) – *Art of Terracotta Cult and Cultural Synthesis in India*, Agam Kala Prakashan, Delhi.

Indigenous Knowledge and Skills of the Bhotiya Women of Uttarkashi

Subhadra Mitra Channa
Professor, Department of Anthropology, University of Delhi, Delhi-110007, India
channa.subhadra@gmail.com

Introduction

Knowledge, away from its elitist definition as something, the acquisition of which confers high status in society, can also be understood as life sustaining practices engaged in by a community over generations. These forms of knowledge with their embodied skills are an aspect of cultural heritage that needs to be cherished as they provide clue to sustainable practices that foster healthy ecological relations. Such forms of knowledge are increasingly being regarded as valuable in light of the present era of environmental problems, many of which are regarded as anthropogenic in nature. The knowledge generated by western science with its emphasis on the domination of nature is now realized to be insufficient to allow this earth to sustain itself for future generations to come. Again in light of feminist theory, this knowledge privileged the masculine perspective by being exploitative and dominating. Rather than fostering co-existence with nature and its resources it sought to put human technology in the service of destruction and war. Over the times, and in the perspective of the current state of global warming and environmental disasters that are occurring with alarming frequency, attention has also turned to the feminine perspectives of nurture and conservation. The indigenous communities with their age old ways and continued and healthy relationships with nature are being re-examined to understand them, not as primitive and backward, as earlier designated but as reservoirs of practical wisdom and sustainable practices and philosophies. In this paper, I will describe the skills and knowledge held by women of a community of traditional sheep herders and horticulturalists on the higher reaches of the Himalayas to show how daily practices learnt through the process of socialization provides an informal body of knowledge that has far reaching value in contributing to life on this earth. Pre-history can thus provide a clue by linking archaeological data to ethnographic observations in search of continuities and to establish linkages between the ancient and contemporary world. By providing a link to understand and assess the antiquity of beliefs and practices it can feed into data that can be used to find solutions to the problem of sustainability, so crucial in the present world. Thus pre-history and archaeology can enrich its possibilities with the help of qualitative data from contemporary societies.

The Bhotiyas

The term Bhotiya is one that is an externally imposed one (Channa 2013) for the community that I am describing here call themselves, Rongpas, and occupy a space near the Gangotri glacier, from which the river Ganga, cascades down to the holy city of Rishikesh but first passing by the small pilgrim town of Uttarkashi. The term Bhotiya is a generic term describing small enclaves of people occupying the fringe villages all along the Himalayan borders (Furer-Haimendorf 1981), that separate the High mountains from the low lands and also the countries of India, Tibet (now China), Nepal and Sikkim. As described in the historical chronicles (Camman 1951, Chauhan 1989, Guha 1989, Joshi 1990), these borders have been changing and have been shifting according to the changing power equations between these countries. The lives of these people have been affected as have their livelihoods as political situations have given rise to changed trade and economic relations and environmental and cultural factors have affected livelihoods.

When studied, in the years 1997-2000, these people, locally and in the official documents, also known as Jad Bhotiyas (Rizvi 1979),[1] had ceased their cross-border trade due to closure of the border with Tibet. Tibet was annexed by China in 1959 and then the consequent war with India and cessation of diplomatic ties destroyed cross –border movements by 1962. The primary occupations left to these people were sheep rearing and processing wool and making and selling of woollen items, weaving carpets, growing of subsistence crops and as a more recent introduction, growing apples as cash crops. While the men also raised animals for transportation and acted as guides, keeping to their travelling lifestyles, trading for example, with Nepal, the women had a lot to contribute to the economy (Channa 2002).

They were transhumant, occupying a higher altitude village near Harsil, a small town on the way to Gangotri town in summer and in winter when this village was submerged in several feet of snow they moved to a lower altitude village, Dunda, near the town of Uttarkashi. They also camped inside the dense forests near Hrishikesh, at a place called Chor-Pani, in winter. At Chor-Pani that was set up as family camps, the horses were brought down to graze and have water, and the people traded in various goods with the local people. They also visited the local villages with rare Himalayan herbs and shrubs. The data for this paper was collected by the ethnographic method, by doing fieldwork, staying in the field and sharing the lives of these people. I was assisted by my students, Anamika Verma and Bhaskar Singh in doing fieldwork, and the Jads were studied in all three locations.

Women's Work and Division of Labour

The women were seen as belonging to the village while the men were seen as rightfully belonging to the wild spaces in their role as herders of sheep and as erstwhile cross-border traders (Channa 2015). The men went away to take the sheep on their year round grazing trips, spanning the entire distance from a point high up above the tree line in summer to the grazing forests near Hrishikesh and Dehradun, in winter, spending most part of the year in travel. The women managed the village, taking care of livestock like horses and goats that stayed in the village, doing horticulture and processing wool and knitting; they also wove carpets. One of their major tasks was to brew beer (*chang)* out of locally grown millets. Their knowledge in all these activities was based upon generations of learning through imitation and contact with their elders and peers. The environment and requirements of day to day lives were an interactive space for creativity as well as continuity. The skills were both learned and individual, for example some women were better at knitting and some at carpet weaving and some at making *chang*. Although, knitting and carpet weaving were both traditional activities, yet they left enough scope for individual creativity and ingenuity for design and style. The women also grew potatoes, maize, red kidney beans and black beans in the small fields surrounding the village.

They also did most of the household work like washing of clothes and utensils and most of the cooking, although the latter was not primarily a woman's task and could be done by a man also. The men had essential knowledge of cooking as they had to cook, when they were away grazing sheep or trekking to do trade. Taking care of babies and children was mostly the task of the elderly, either men or women and so was that of spinning wool. One could see older men and women, with a baby slung on their back, and a spinning wheel in their hand roaming the village. Often one found a grandfather or grandmother putting a baby to sleep. The tasks that involved physical hard work were done by the young to middle aged men and women.

The life of a woman was hard. They began to work by imitating their mothers, when they were as young as three or four and continued to work till such time as they could move their hands and feet. While men often retired to laze about the village, playing dice or just sleeping in the sun, it was rare to find even a very old woman doing nothing. During my stay in the village I would get up in the morning to find most women gone to the fields or to the forest. One could see a small girl tagging

[1] In this paper they will be referred to as 'Jads' as this is the name by which they are most widely recognized.

along with her mother as she went to wash clothes or to wash her vessels in the downstream near the end of the village. This little girl would be given a few small clothes or dishes to wash and one could see them proudly carrying these in their tiny hands as they came back to the village. Even as one could see young boys playing cricket or lounging around girls of as young as eight were chopping wood or cooking or beating wool. The women consequently grew up more responsible and most of the important tasks like arranging for a wedding or a ritual were done by them. The men took instructions and rarely tried to impose themselves, keeping to the background, as the general belief was that the village belonged to women and men were for the wild (Channa 2015).

The women's work could be primarily divided into the following tasks

1. Household work
2. Cultivation in the fields
3. Processing of wool and making knitted woollen items
4. Making *Chang*
5. Going to the forest to collect fire wood, fodder and minor forest products.
6. Performance of household and other rituals

Each of these involved skills and also knowledge about the environment, some of it involving the knowledge of cosmological significance.

Let us examine them one by one.

Household work

This involves cooking and cleaning and the optimum use of naturally available resources, especially water. The food cooked is mostly rice and some vegetables but mostly lentils, like red kidney beans or black lentils that grow in this region. Although the Jads are not vegetarian and relish meat, they never slaughter their own animals. Only if an animal dies accidently, like falling off a cliff, is it eaten. Otherwise even to make a sacrifice, they will buy one from the market. The Jad men will never wield a knife to kill any animal but sacrifice or butchering is done by men of a low caste (Khatik) who are butchers by profession. Each household has a hearth in the kitchen that is fuelled by wood as coal is rarely found here. The higher altitudes do not have any domestic gas connections as no cylinders can be delivered to this remote are, far away from the main road and which is hidden behind forests and mountain streams. The men and women both know how to keep this hearth going and how to light it. These hearths made of iron are of very great antiquity and used for generations in the same way. They also sometimes have chimneys that take the smoke away out of the house but mostly they are open and in the centre of a large kitchen where food is also eaten. The women also have to stock up for the winter months and most houses have a storage space with logs piled up in bundles. Fodder for the animals and some food is also stored by drying specific herbs and nuts.

The use of water is also controlled to optimize its use for various purposes and to minimize wastage. The village is located on the side of wild streams that are the tributaries of the river Ganga, as it flows down from the Go-Mukh glacier. This water is used only for occasional ritual baths and is considered sacred. For their daily uses they have a canal running through the back of the village that channels water from a mountain stream. As this canal enters the village, it is guarded by the village deity, Me-Parang, who, represented by long poles and red cloth, stands at the entrance to the village and the stream flows past, from behind him to enter the habitation. The households of the upper caste Rongpas[2] are right next to the flowing stream and they can use the water flowing behind their houses for cooking and drinking but all villagers must go down stream towards the bottom of the village for

[2] The Jads are divided into two ranked groups with the Chiang holding a higher position than the Phiba. The village is organized in such a way that the Chiang occupy the houses near the main road that divides the village into two halves and have the nearest access to water and the village entrance.

cleaning their household vessels and for washing clothes. Thus upstream water is used as potable water for human consumption and downstream water as a cleaning agent.

There are many mountain streams in this region and while in the forest they can use his water but it has to be done sparingly and with caution. Any stream flowing out of the mountainside that faces the sun is considered sacred and as the abode of the *naga devta* or snake god. No one must defile such a stream and even if one can quench one's thirst, one must not wash anything dirty in it, nor perform any defiling act near it. Any such defilement causes the person to be cursed with disease and bad dreams. I was told many stories of first hand experiences of people who had broken the taboos and had been troubled by boils erupting on the body or bad dreams, and sometimes they found a cure by a shaman but sometimes they had to live with it.

Cultivation in the fields

Earlier in time, before 1961, when the Jads had some land near their inhabited villages at Neilang and Jadung, higher up and nearer the Indo-Tibet border, they practiced some plough cultivation growing rice, with the help of mountain cows and yaks. After the closure of the border when these two villages were relocated to Harsil, the plough cultivation almost stopped as the yaks were also difficult to raise at the lower altitude. There was also not enough land. In more recent times they have been mostly growing potatoes and barley in the high altitude village and red beans and black lentils in the lower altitude village along with a little rice. Most of the work of preparing the fields, weeding, sowing, cutting canals for irrigation and harvesting is done by the women. Sometimes the women hire lower caste men from other villages to do some of the work for them, but the men of high Rongpa lineages do not cultivate. Women mostly work alone in the fields, but help each other out when work gets to too much to handle. The older women may also supervise the younger ones in doing some of these tasks, and as one young woman remarked, a mother-in-law is never satisfied with the work that her haughtier-in-law does. But work teams usually comprise of sisters and women of similar age, who can also get along with each other. In doing cultivation, they often take turns to help and social network are always seen as an important resource. Cosmologically women are compared to milk that flows and builds relations.

Processing of Wool and Knitting

The wool is sheared by the men in the forests near the habitations and then handed over to the women for processing. The raw wool is rarely sold. The men may however sell the male sheep to others, if there is a surplus. The wool is then processed in several steps to make it into skeins that can be knitted or woven. The very first step is cleaning, for this the wool is spread on hides and then beaten with long sticks, about four feet in length. It is a laborious process in which the woman sits on her haunches and used two sticks to beat the wool with both hands, sometimes for 2-hours or more. A little girl from the age of about six is given smaller sticks to beat the wool and this is the first thing she learns to do. The beaten wool is then passed through a comb to clean it. The wooden comb is passed over the wool spread on a square wooden frame with a wire mesh so that the impurities get sieved off the wool. This work is done mostly by adult women or even elderly women as it does not require much strength but only skill. The cleaned wool is then dyed. The wool comes in three natural colours, white, black and grey and it is dyed into a rich brown or warm yellow with locally available vegetable dyes. The beautiful brown comes from walnuts, of which, the kernel are first eaten and the shells spread over a piece of cloth to dry in the sun. A soft shell separates from the hard woody outer shell, and this is then boiled in water to produce the brown dye. The yellow/orange colour is obtained from the pollen of the deodar trees, although this is rarely used in clothes or shawls that are worn but mostly used to dye wool that is woven into carpets. The cleaned and dyed wool is then spun into skeins either on the traditional spindle held in the hand or on a modern spindle that operates as a sewing machine with the feet. Older women and men; were mostly using the traditional spindle at the time when this fieldwork was conducted. The machine spindle, provided by the state, was being used by the younger women. Men never used it.

Knitting is done by the women. A little girl about five or six is allowed to fiddle with wool and someone may teach her to cast on a few stitches. Most girls become expert knitter by the time they get to the age of twelve or so. The Jads have an unwritten rule that only the person who makes any article has the right to sell it. This means that many times young girls make knitted items like stockings, caps and gloves and then sell them in the local market for money that they can keep and use as they please. This makes the young girls quite independent from an early age.

The women do not however weave the wool which is handed to the lower caste Koli, who also occupy the marginal lower space of the Jad village. They weave the wool into shawls on looms that are taboo for use by the Bhotiya community. The woven shawls are handed over to the Jads again for selling in the market, and the Kolis get a small fee for their work. Although women do not weave, they have ownership over a piece by having processed the wool by which it is made. Thus I was often told while negotiating price for a shawl that it belongs to such and such woman, and only she can tell the price.

The women weave beautiful carpets and it is considered the most highly skilled of all the work that they can do. While most other work is done while sitting in a group and talking and gossiping, weaving a carpet is done individually and the weaver does not speak for she has to keep counting the threads in her head.

The workspace for most activities like beating the wool, knitting, combing, dyeing and spinning is in the common areas of the village, where a number of women come together, weaving a carpet is done in the seclusion of a room or *verandah*, away from everyone else. Not many women weave carpets, but those who do, can get a good price for it. The motifs are inspired by Chinese motifs of dragons and flowers etc. These are mostly taken to Chor-pani and sold from there.

Making Chang

This is seen as one of the most important skills of a woman and not every woman is a good maker of millet beer, just like every woman is not highly skilled in all activities like knitting and weaving o carpets. But *chang* is a social requirement without which the social and ritual life of the Bhotiyas remains incomplete. Both men and women drink large quantities of it at functions like marriage and other rituals that mark births, deaths and possession rituals and séance. The millets are collected in large vessels, fermented with locally available yeasts collected from the forests, distilled and stored in various kinds of vessels. At any wedding one can see a long row of women coming with bottles and other vessels of all kind carrying *chang*. They pour it into a common large cask from which then everyone can have as much as they can, while it lasts. I have often heard women discuss the finer nuances of *chang* making with each other and sometimes one who is viewed as an expert will be asked to make *chang* for a special occasion in someone else's house.

Visiting the forests for minor forest produce

The Jads recognize two kinds of forests, those that are near their habitations, known as *regas* and those that the on the far away high mountains called *danda*. The women are tabooed from going to the far away forests and for this reason cannot graze animals like goats and sheep that have to be taken on their long pastoral routes only by the men. The women can visit the *rega*, for minor forest produce like fuel wood, fodder for the house animals and also a number of berries, leaves and mushrooms to be eaten; they can also identify medicinal plants of which they have a vast storehouse of knowledge. They collect a fragrant herb called *shukwa* that is used as incense in their rituals and also the pollen of the deodar flowers that also has ritual use parallel to that of turmeric in the Hindu culture. I have often seen women carry back leaves and small plants that are added to the menu for the day. But what they really need to carry and store is firewood by collecting dry twigs and small branches of the tree. They go barehanded with only a small cutting knife and do not cut any trees. Each woman returns from a full day of collecting firewood bent over double with a huge bundle that may be 30-40 Kilograms. The bundle is carried by a strap passing over their back and head holding it in place. Because the women carry such heavy loads, they wear a special item of clothing called a *paagri*, that is a long piece of cloth about seven feet in length and three feet in width, that is tied around their stomachs and waist like a wide band. This is supposed to protect her internal organs from damage while she carries heavy loads up and down the mountain side. Every full grown woman of all ages wears it all the time. This is woven for them by the Koli weavers. The Jad women do not cover their heads like the local Garhwali women but have a piece of cloth also wound about the head, which is also used for tying up loads when required. The nurse practitioner at the local clinic told me that the Jad women rarely suffer miscarriages and do not have severe gynaecological problems. But my interviews with the women revealed that they do suffer from reproductive disorders and several reported having had hysterectomies done. But overall they seemed well equipped to handle the tough lifestyle and whatever health related issues they had did not apparently stem from their work. More important for them is to be protected from the forest spirits called Matriyal who are very jealous of humans and tend to harm them. For this reason the Jads do not wear bright coloured clothes when in the high altitudes. This is also why the wool that is knitted for clothes is not dyed any bright colours. They feel that the forest spirits get jealous if they see someone looking beautiful and a good looking man or woman is advised to smear their face with mud if they are going into the forest.

The deodar trees in the forest are each treated as *deota* (god), and the flowers are treated as sacred. A person while going to the forest should behave as one entering a holy place like one enters a temple. One should tread softly, talk in whispers, never throw dirt and never carry out any inappropriate action like defecation or sexual intercourse, while in the forest. A menstruating woman must not enter the forest and women are careful not to go to the forest on days when they expect the onset of their periods.

This reverence for forests and its resources has led to centuries of sustainable relationship with the environment, but one that is now threatened by the onslaught of the external world. The region belonging to the Jads is somewhat protected because of its strategic military significance. The army maintains the dense forest cover for its own protection. The traditional right s of the Jads to their higher altitude pastures is recognized and they have special passes to graze in those areas although their villages have been relocated.

The ritual role of the women

The Jads consider men to be ritually superior to women just as they consider nature to be superior to culture (Channa 2015). Their main rituals involve the lineage gods or *kuldevta*, who are passed down the male line from father to son. Although ideally it is the men who are supposed to be performing rituals, in actual terms it is women who have to do it, as traditionally the men are away on their trade and other activities. In the present times, the men (and some women also) have also become educated and jobs in the cities and are hence away from the village. In their cognitive map, the Jads equate the city with the wilderness (Channa 2010) and women rarely accompany the men to their places of work. Their role is to stay in the village and take care of the social, economic, ritual and political life of the village. The *kuldevta* have to be made daily offerings but periodic offerings are also made to the village deity, Meparang, who, already described, stands at the entrance to the village. The women's role also lies in collecting resources, pooling a work force, make co-operative units to deal with different aspects of the rituals and in general to organize and administer. Ultimately they feel responsible for the carrying out of all ritual tasks and for the welfare of the village. For example many housewives make offerings in the morning to the souls of sixty persons who died when their bus crashed into the deep crevice that separates their village from the main road. They feel that the persons, who died an unnatural and untimely death, may come to haunt their village and it is their duty to take preventive action. I have witnessed women organizing possession rituals to solicit the aid of the Pandavas (Channa 2005) to seek help for the health of their daughters or others. Women often take initiative creatively to organize a ritual that may not be part of the usual repertoire; but the people of the village may participate or may be sceptical, but no one questions her right to do so.

The Continuity of Traditions and their Relevance

Although not much material is available regarding the archaeology of this region, yet the presence of the Bhotiyas, or people inhabiting the strategic regions near the Himalayan passes (The Jads occupy the region near the Neilang pass) to carry on cross border-trade and also to act as porter and guides for pilgrims on these routes has been recorded for many centuries. Naithani (1986:180) mentions that the main cause of the relationship of Tibet with ancient India was the Kailas-Mansoravar pilgrimage that drew Hindus from the plains of India to this far flung region, and that the border communities like the Bhotiyas played a key role in facilitating these journeys. The presence of Mongoloid looking people referred as Khas or Khasa also finds mention in the ancient texts (Allen 1997:304). However most of the accounts describe the masculine activities of trade and commerce and travel, there is no mention of women and their activities in these early historical and ethnographical texts.

As we have seen in this paper, the women play a significant role in the adaptation of the community to the environment and in the preservation and conservation of local resources. The local cosmology and belief patterns on which this conservation is largely dependent is nurtured by women as the men are more open to outside influences. The Jad dichotomy between the masculine and feminine world makes this all the more significant as the women are the ones viewed as *responsible* as the ones having a stake in the environment and in the continuity of the life worlds that sustain these resources. Even as the men made themselves conspicuous by their spectacular trade and commercial activities sometimes even engaging in war, the women resolutely carried on with their day to day activities, sustaining their lives and that of others in their vicinity. Among the Jads there is a taboo on women killing or even breaking something as they are seen as life giving and life nurturing.

Prehistoric data analysis primarily depends on technological aspects of imaging and chemical analysis, but a lot can be gained by supplementing these kinds of objective data by the ethnographic accounts of contemporary communities, that still engage in the ancient life-ways like pastoralism and still make use of natural resources from their primary sources like forests and mountain streams, like the Jads. The immense knowledge of these women about the bounties yielded by the natural forest, about the climate and sounds and sights of the landscape is a treasure house that may well be lost if enough attention is not paid to it and that can only be done if one recognizes the environmental significance in terms of sustainability of these forms of indigenous knowledge. It is also important to understand the gendered aspect of indigenous knowledge. For the last hundred years or so, the entire scholarship about this region has focussed on the men's activities and these communities have been named and defined as 'cross-border traders' or 'sheep-herders' etc; based on the work done by the men (Bora 1996, Brown 1994). The focus on women brings out the less spectacular dimensions of indigenous knowledge and subsistence activities that might throw greater light on both the past and the possible future of these communities.

References

Allen, N. J. (1997) – 'Hinduization: The Experience of the Thulung Rai' In David N Gellner, Joanna Pfaff-Czarnecka, and John Whelpton (eds), *Asian Highland Societies in Anthropological Perspective*. New Delhi: Sterling Publishers, pp. 168-202.

Bora, R. S. (1996) – *Himalayan Migration: A Study of the Hill Region of Uttar Pradesh,* New Delhi: Sage Publications.

Brown, C. W. (1994) – 'Salt, Barley, Pashmina and Tincal-Contexts of Being Bhotiya in Traiil's Kumaon', In M. P. Joshi, Allen Fonger, and C.W. Brown (eds.), *The Himalaya: Past and Present*, Almora: Shree Almora Book Dept, pp. 147-71.

Camman, S. V. R. (1951) – *Trade through the Himalayas: The Early British Attempts to Open Tibet*, Princeton: Princeton University Press.

Channa, S. M. (2002) – 'The Life History of a Jad Woman' *European Bulletin of Himalayan Research*, 22 (Spring):61-81.

Channa, S. M. (2005) – 'The Descent of the Pandavas', *European Bulletin of Himalayan Research*, 28 (Spring): 67-87.

Channa, S. M. (2010) – 'The Wilderness of the Civilization' in Marie Lecomte-Tilouine (ed,), *An Exploration of the Categories of Nature and Culture in Asia and the Himalayas*, New Delhi: Social Science Press, pp. 222-44.

Channa, S. M. (2013) – *The Inner and Outer Selves: Cosmology, Gender, and Ecology at the Himalayan Borders*, New Delhi: Oxford University Press.

Channa, S. M. (2015) – 'Men as Nature and Women as Culture: Women's Work and Reproduction of a Pastoral Community on the Himalayan Borders' In Subhadra Mitra Channa and Marilyn Porter (eds) *Gender, Livelihood and Environment: How Women Manage Resources*, New Delhi: Orient Blackswan, pp. 1-20.

Chauhan, R. S. (1989) – *Society and State Building in Nepal: From Ancient Times to Mid-Twentieth Century.* South Asia Studies Series, 20, New Delhi: Sterling Publishers.

Furer-Haimendorf, Christoph von (1981) – *Asian Highland Societies in Anthropological Perspective*, New Delhi: Sterling Publishers.

Guha, R. (1989) – *The Unquiet Woods: Ecological Change and Peasant Resistance in the Himalaya*, New Delhi: Oxford University Press.

Joshi, M. P. (1990) – *Uttaranchal Himalaya (Kumaon-Garhwal) – An Essay in Historical Anthropology*. Almora: Shree Almora Book Depot.

Naithani, S. P. (1986) – 'Ancient Garhwal in Historical Perspective' in N. R. Roy (ed) *Himalayan Frontiers in Historical Perspective*. Calcutta: Institute of Historical Studies, pp. 175-83.

Rawat, A. S. (1983) – *Garhwal Himalayas, A Historical Survey: Poliical and Administrative History of Garhwal, 1815- 1947.* Delhi: Eastern Book Linkers.

Rizvi, S. A. (1979) – *Uttarkashi: Uttar Pradesh District Gazeteer,* Vol. 18. Lucknow: Govt. Of Uttarpradesh, Department of District Gazeteers, Uttar Pradesh.

Mask of Chhau – A Tribal Heritage through the Ages in West Bengal: An Ethno-Archaeological Study in Charida Group of People

Banani Bhattacharyya
The Ramkrishna Mission Institute of Culture,
Centre for Indological Studies & Research, Kolkata, India
banani303@yahoo.co.in

Introduction

A mask is an important part of theatre craft that is worn normally for performance in dramas or plays, or for amusement. Masks have been used since antiquity for both ceremonial and practical purposes. Tradition of West Bengal allows the artists to wear masks made of various materials among which wood plays an important role. Chhau dance is a mask-dance which represents characteristics of primitive ritualistic dance in its vigour, style and musical accompaniment. Wood masks in West Bengal are the creations of the artisans who with their exclusive use of cuttings and colours give the masks a touch of their originality. Masks are believed to embody the spirit of an ancestor, and symbolize a message of wisdom, prosperity, security, and power. It has been worn in cultures throughout the world for thousands of years. These are made of varied materials including paper, cloth, grass, leather, metal, wood and stone. They are painted with symbolic designs and vivid colours. Masks and their manifold forms are a very significant mode of cultural expression. The masks generally made here are of mythological character and the material used is paper mache painted in bright colours. Today Masks are more popular as items of interior decoration.

The craft of mask making in West Bengal is closely related to the folk-dance forms. And musks are generally prepared during the months of January- February until the Chaitra-Baisakh Gajan Festival, which is the peak season of Chauu dance. These masks made of clay; wood and paper are used in the performance of *Chhau*, a traditional dance of West Bengal. The masks are mainly of Puranic characters, gods, goddesses and animals.

The Chhau region is a tribal tract of eastern India and had as its original inhabitants, indigenous tribes like the Santhal, Munda, Ho, Oraon, Gond, Bhuiyan, Bhumij and Kol to name a few. Over a sustained

Figure 1 & 2. Masks

period of time, spanning many centuries people from other parts of the country settled here. This led to an intermingling of the local tribal culture with that of the migratory population. The communities that now constitute a large part of the present day population are mostly of this mixed descent and are associated with Chhau as Gurus/ Ustads or teachers, performers, musicians, instrument makers, mask-makers and costume/ ornament makers. These are detailed as under:

1. The dance aspect is mainly practised by the communities known as Mundas, Mahatos, Kalindis, Pattnaiks, Samals, Darogas, Mohantys, Acharyas, Bhols, Kars, Dubeys, and Sahoos.
2. The musical accompaniment is provided to Chhau Dance by people of communities known as Mukhis, Kalindis, Ghadheis, Dhada. They are also involved in the making of the instruments.
3. As masks form an integral part of Chhau Dance in Purulia and Seraikella the craft of mask making involves communities of traditional painters known as Maharanas, Mohapatras and Sutradhars.
   a. A craftsman making a clay model from which moulds will be taken.
   b. Three stages of making a Chhau mask.
   c. Masks of male and female tribal characters in the Chhau dance.
   d. Mask of a tiger made in Charida in Purulia district.

Purulia district of West Bengal is a place where masks are found in huge variety especially wood masks. The wooden masks of west Bengal have become a popular theatre craft, admired for its simplicity. The wooden mask makers are generally the wood-carvers by caste. The artisans for 'chhou' masks are mostly located in and around Charida and Bagmundi of Purulia district. The masks of hilly areas is carved out of soft wood and painted vividly with subtle use of bright colours representing the evil spirits of the mountains and the demons. The performer wears a mask, purified by mantras; dances with a sword, and makes prophetic answers. This art depends fully on the local Chhau dance of Purulia. Earlier the masks were made out of Simul wood and considering the poverty of local dancers, the cheap materials were introduced later. The paper describes historical background, material used, traditional methods of preparation and cultural significance of masks and also highlights the musicological, psychological and philosophical significance of these masks and focused description of the *Chhau* masks of Charida, West Bengal.

In Bengal, masks actually represent the theatrical tradition are used by the Chhou dancers of Purulia. The masks generally made here are of mythological character and the material used is paper

FIGURE 3. PEOPLE DANCING WITH MASKS

mache painted in bright colours. Today Masks are more popular as items of interior decoration. A mask is an important part of theatre craft that is worn normally for performance in dramas or plays, or for amusement. Masks have been used since antiquity for both ceremonial and practical purposes. The culture and tradition of West Bengal allows the artists to wear masks made of various materials among which wood plays an important role. Wood masks in West Bengal are the creations of the artisans who with their exclusive use of cuttings and colours give the masks a touch of their originality.

Mask, used since antiquity for both ceremonial and practical purposes, are normally worn on the face, typically for protection, concealment, performance, or amusement. Masks are believed to embody the spirit of an ancestor, and symbolize a message of wisdom, prosperity, security, and power. Masks have been worn in cultures throughout the world for thousands of years. Masks are made of varied materials including paper, cloth, grass, leather, metal, wood and stone. They are painted with symbolic designs and vivid colours. Masks and their manifold forms are a very significant mode of cultural expression. The article also highlights the musicological, psychological and philosophical significance of these masks and focused description of the *Chhau* masks of West Bengal. There are a number of explanations for the derivation of the name 'Chhau'. The word is believed by certain people to come from the Sanskrit root 'Chhaya', meaning shadow. As masks are an integral feature of this dance, it is thence called 'Chhau', which means mask. Some people believe it is derived from the local word 'chho' which means expressing or doing something with gestures. Another explanation is that long ago this dance was performed by the military of the local kingdom in their leisure time. The themes included their heroic deeds and traditional folklore. They performed this dance for their own entertainment as well as to encourage themselves. As it was performed in their camps (locally known as 'Chhauni'), the name 'Chhau' came from that term.

Purulia district of West Bengal is a place where masks are found in huge variety especially wood masks. The wooden masks of west Bengal have become a popular theatre craft, admired for its simplicity. The wooden mask makers are generally the wood-carvers by caste and are located in two or three centres in Purulia. They were also acknowledged as 'Dutta' and 'Seal'. This art depend fully

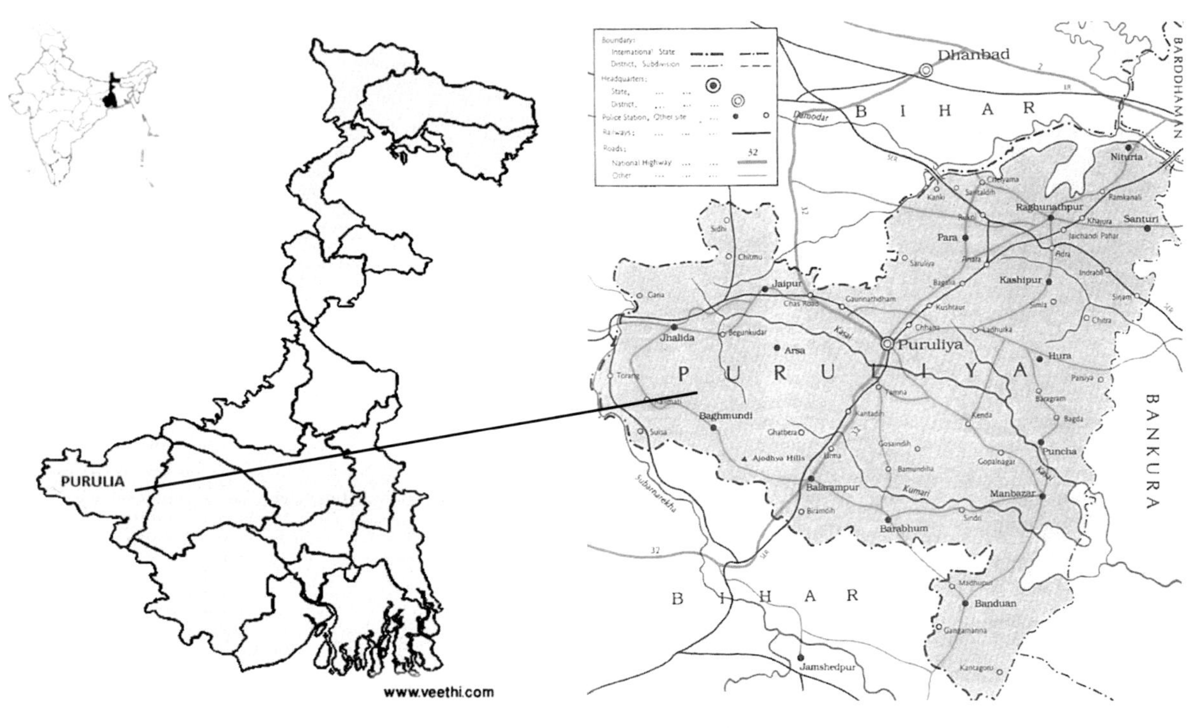

Figure 4. Location of purulia in West Bengal, India

Figure 5. Area of Baghmundi, Purulia

Figure 6. Dance of Chhau, Purulia

on the local Chhau dance of Purulia. Chhau dance is a mask-dance which represents characteristics of primitive ritualistic dance in its vigour, style and musical accompaniment. Earlier the masks were made out of Simul wood and considering the poverty of local dancers, the cheap materials were introduced later.

Around 250 artisans from 60-70 families, mostly belong to the Sutradhar clan, are engaged in making these extraordinarily beautiful masks for generations. The mask-maker needs extremely high artistic perfection and the detailed knowledge of the epic and mythology is also essential to express the shade of a particular character.

FIGURE 7. VIEW OF BAGHMUNDI, WAY TO CHARIDA

FIGURE 8. GENERAL VIEW OF VILLAGE CHARIDA

The most notable feature of the Chhau is the dresses and masks. Some villagers are completely dedicated to the task. Here, almost every person is an expert on the making of masks and dresses. Children are trained in the forms of the dance from a young age. Chhau involves a display of physical skills, exercise and immensely hard work.

FIGURE 9. PEOPLE WORKING ON MASKS

FIGURE 10. PEOPLE WORKING ON MASKS

- The masks generally made here are of mythological character.
- Chhau masks became an indispensable element of Chhau dance. As it is impossible for the artist to show mood variations through facial expressions, the expression in the mask's face is very important to illustrate different moods.
- Purulia Chhau uses masks, and in addition it exhibits the spontaneity of folk art. It was sustained and developed by the people themselves.

Materials and methods

The craft of these mask is closely related to the folk dance forms. These are generally prepared during the month of Fagun, January-February until the Chaitra-Baisakh, Gajan Festival, which is the peak season of Chhau dance. The craft of mask making along with Chhau dance has been a tradition here for well over a century. The Chhau dance has qualities similar to a primitive ceremonial dance, reflected in the masks.

Masks depicting characters from mythological stories, various gods and goddesses, animals, birds, demons, tribal men-women are made.

Earlier they made masks out of Simul wood considering the poverty of local dancers, the cheap materials were introduced later and the decoration was simple. The paper describes historical background, material used, traditional methods of preparation and cultural significance of masks and also highlights the musicological, psychological and philosophical significance of these masks and focused description of the *Chhau* masks of Charida, West Bengal. The culture and tradition of West Bengal allows the artists to wear masks made of various materials among which wood plays an important role. Wood masks in West Bengal are the creations of the artisans who with their exclusive use of cuttings and colours give the masks a touch of their originality.

Conclusion

Chhau is a performing art of dance and music which is intimately connected to Chaitra-Parva, the festival of spring celebrated in April every year. This has a special significance to the art through the rituals connected with it. The festival lasts for thirteen days in which the whole community

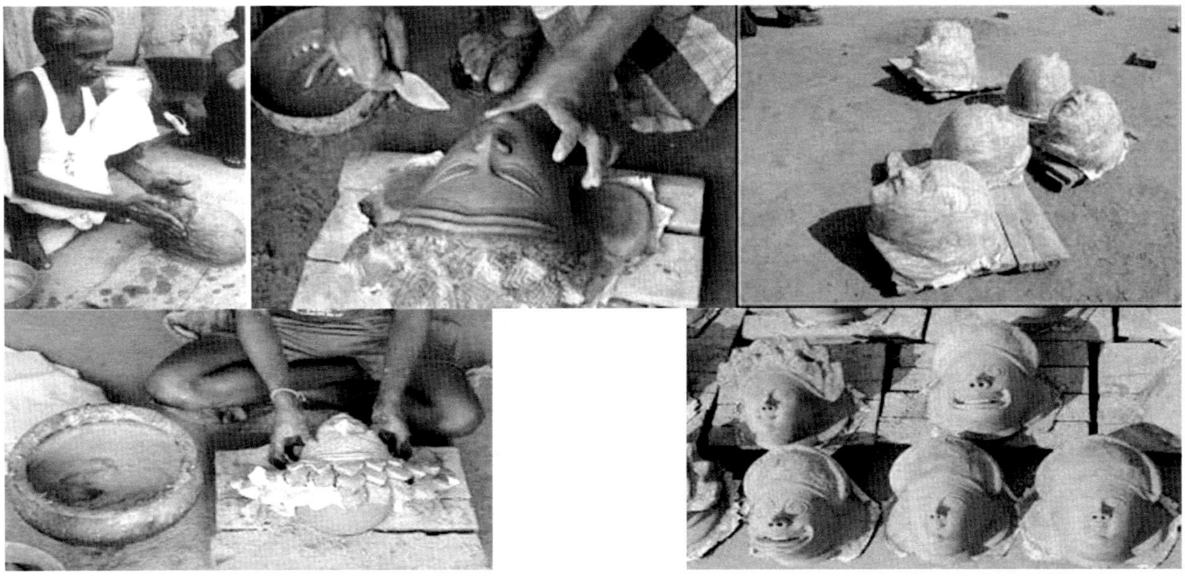

FIGURE 11. CLAY MODEL OF THE MASK IS MADE, OVER WHICH LAYERS OF WASTE PAPER AND RAGS ARE PASTED AND THEN DRIED

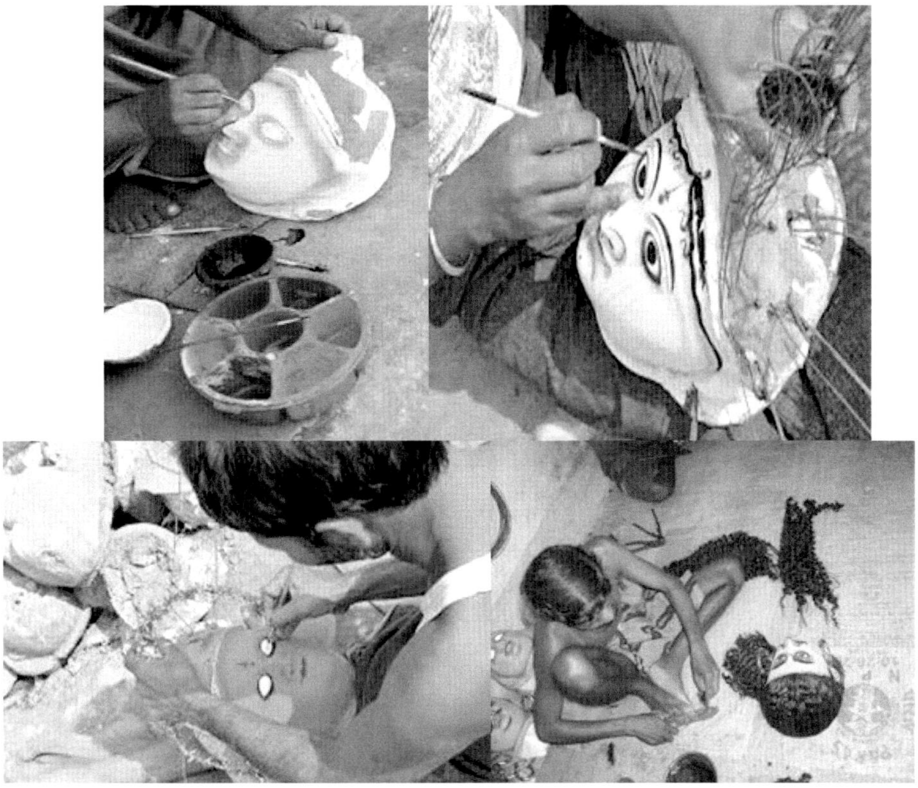

Figure 12. Process of painting the mask

Figure 13. Final stage is decoration of the mask

participates. The usage of stylized masks is an important component of Purulia *Chhau* dance. This requires skilled craftsmanship which has also evolved as an art in itself and is being preserved by its community.

Chhau are performed with masks. The dancer aims to animate the mask through the movements of the body. The masks give a larger-than-life feel to the characters and imbue them with a mythical quality. They are invariably integrated with ornate headgears that give them a resplendent touch. The performance traditionally takes place through the night in an open-air arena called Akhada or Asar which is sanctified and decorated. The audience is seated in a circular manner all around the Akhada. The dance is preceded by a traditional rhythm played on the drums known as Judon in Purulia.

Figure 14. Workshop of Manaranjan Sutradhar, Charida

Figure 15. Aswini Sutradhar, one of the oldest artisan of the area

This is a ritual offering for an auspicious beginning to the patron deities and creates the proper aesthetic mood for the performance. Chhau is an integral part of the core culture of these communities and contributes greatly towards their identity. This is the reason that despite poor economic conditions it is still being sustained by the people of this region.

Besides its importance to culture, Chhau is crucial to the local economy. There is a global audience for this folk art form, and a large number of families earn their livelihood by performing and selling masks and dresses. But the future does not look bright, as a lack of care, an absence of planning for the business of Chhau and government apathy threaten its growth. Fewer young people are willing to take up Chhau given the financial uncertainties that surround it. They prefer to look for jobs that don't have so much uncertainty. The only way to ensure the long-term future of this art would be to make those involved in it financially secure.

Figure 16. Remains of their earlier craftsmanship

The whole world is searching the answer of the dichotomy between 'tradition' and 'modernity'; what will be the choice between the options of 'folk heritage' and 'popular culture'?

The dichotomy in front of us is the powerful cultural heritage on the one hand and modernity on the other. Standing within the frame of the ideology of pluralism, we must be able to establish a strong interactive relationship between modernity and tradition. We can use folk- art form as the tools for this. Timely reforms are the very spirit of folk-arts. These art forms took shape based on caste, religion and ethnic boundaries. In the world of today where individual revaluation and global civilization become challenges to national identity, micro cultures will survive only if cultural pluralism is retained.

The protection and nourishment of folk arts is the means to it. Indian society is undergoing an acute culture crisis; which is reflected by the traditional community organizations being suppressed under severe moral, social and economic pressure.

Standing within the frame of ideology of pluralism, the social scientists and researcher have to endeavour to establish a strong interactive relationship between tradition and modernity. Society and culture – both are dynamic entity; it is usual for society and cultural characteristics to be modified with time. Besides, the process of assimilation of valuable social and cultural features enriches the society and culture. Effort of updating, revision and refinement of folk forms are desirable to benefit it with time; but it should be restricted to a limit, beyond which the folk cultures may be 'sold' to the popular cultures.

Under such circumstances it can be say for ensuring the prevention of Chhau as a tribal/folk art and culture:

- Commercialization of Chhau as folk art and culture for their profitable running is one of the instrumental ways to survive the folk forms;
- Conservation of their innate beauty, inherent quality and core ideology is essential;
- People are required to be informed with the values, styles, forms of this performing art. Effective campaigning and publicity of these elements may actualize a mass attraction towards folk art and culture;

- The colleges and universities in corresponding areas should incorporate this particular dance form as respective course of studies;
- However, the tribal / folk artists and cultural practitioners themselves should also upgrade their skill with the current socio-economic and socio-cultural trend of the broader society.
- While formulating the creative compositions like folklores community song & dance etc. these artists should modify the content of composition or pattern of expression in order to gratify the need and demand of the common people of the community as well as broader society.
- The performers of the Chhau should continually upgrade their creative flair and operational skill so that they themselves can play a proactive role in bolstering the foundation and ensuring the sustainability of Tribal / Folks Arts and Culture. They should adopt a proactive stance in carrying the rich cultural legacy of India and proceed forward in pursuit of functional excellence.